Evaluating Your Liturgical Music Ministry

Keith L. Patterson

Resource Publications, Inc.
San Jose, California

Editorial director: Kenneth Guentert
Managing editor: Elizabeth J. Asborno
Cover design and production: Huey Lee

Reprint Department
Resource Publications, Inc.
160 E. Virginia Street #290
San Jose, CA 95112-5876.

Library of Congress Cataloging in Publication Data
Patterson, Keith L., 1949-
Evaluating your liturgical music ministry / Keith L. Patterson.
p. cm.
Includes bibliographical references.
ISBN 0-89390-258-6 : $19.95
1. Church music—Catholic church—Evaluation. I. Title.
MT88.P35 1993
264'.0202—dc20 92-44562

97 96 95 94 93 | 5 4 3 2 1

For you, Eugene. Your intelligence, wit and genuine human warmth colored everything you wrote, and painted for us a wonderful vision of what we and our liturgies *can* be. May we live the dream.

Contents

APPENDICES: Forms and Instructions

Acknowledgments

Grateful acknowledgment is extended for permission to reprint the following copyrighted material:

Excerpts from the English translation of *The Roman Missal* © 1973, International Committee on English in the Liturgy, Inc. (ICEL); excerpts from the English translation of *Documents on the Liturgy, 1963-1979: Conciliar, Papal, and Curial Texts* © 1982, ICEL. All rights reserved.

Excerpts from "The Milwaukee Symposia for Church Composers: A Ten Year Report" © 1992 Archdiocese of Milwaukee. All rights reserved.

Excerpts taken from **Music in Catholic Worship** Copyright © 1983 by the United StatesCatholic Conference, 3211 Fourth Street, N.E., Washington, D.C. 20017-1194 are used with permission. All rights reserved.

Introduction

THERE'S AN APOCRYPHAL story about Ed Koch, former mayor of New York. It is said that he would go for walks, stopping strangers along the way and saying, "Hi, I'm Ed Koch, mayor of this city. How'm I doin'?" It was a habit that endeared him to the people and provided him a way to determine what his constituency thought about the job he was doing.

Feedback is the key to growth in any system. If you want to improve what you're doing, you have to have a starting reference point. We *all* need to ask "How'm I doin'?" from time to time—even liturgical musicians.

That is the purpose of this book: to provide a technique for obtaining a "snapshot" of the state of your liturgical music program at any given time so you can see where you are in relation to where you want to be. It also provides a mechanism

I urge you to read at least the primary background documents from which the Standards have been culled. They are The Constitution on the Sacred Liturgy, Music in Catholic Worship, Liturgical Music Today, and The General Instruction of the Roman Missal.

for recording selections over the course of a year so you can more easily evaluate choices which span the course of a season or a year.

Part One of this book discusses the standards upon which this evaluation model is based. Part Two explains how to go about the process, providing the "nuts and bolts" of this feedback system. The Appendices provide tools with which to measure attainment of the standards (you must be familiar with the standards before you can make effective use of the tools).

This book is written primarily with the liturgical music director in mind. It provides an analytical tool that can be used to determine the strengths and weaknesses of the music program—the musicians and their performances, the worship environment and resources, the process by which songs and hymns are selected. Information obtained by using this system provides an accurate picture of the program and opens the door to suggestions for improvement.

Members of a parish ministry team (other than a music director) may wish to use this system as well. For instance, an ensemble or folk group may wonder if they are making good musical and liturgical choices and presenting the material in such a way as to enhance the worship experience of the assembly. A liturgy committee, a pastor, or a parish without a music director may wish to assess the state of their liturgical music program but feel inadequate to the task. This system puts into their hands a simple yet effective tool for accomplishing that.

We've come a long way since the 1960s, when The Constitution on the Sacred Liturgy was published. It seemed that overnight we were caught up in a rush to implement the changes suggested by that document. There didn't seem to be a plan or a preparation for the changes. They just "happened" to us.

Since then, guiding documents such as Music in Catholic Worship, Liturgical Music Today, and a revised General Instruction of the Roman Missal have been published, as well as a plethora of educational and insightful articles and books. Liturgical music conferences and seminars abound locally, regionally and nationally. There's no excuse for not knowing "what's going on" and "what's expected of me" any more.

What *is* missing is a simple-to-use evaluation model that can be used from time to time to help those who are responsible for selection and execution of liturgical music to focus on the basics and to provide a "reality check" on their choices. This book fills that void (or so go the author's hopes).

I've written this text in a relaxed, informal style, but I have also provided extensive notes for those who may wish to research the material further. Though not necessary for understanding this book, if you are a seriously involved liturgical musician, I urge you to read at least the primary background documents from which the Standards have been culled. They are The Constitution on the Sacred Liturgy, Music in Catholic Worship, Liturgical Music Today, and The General Instruction of the Roman Missal.

Although not a "guiding document" in the same sense as those cited above, I commend to you the "Milwaukee Symposia for Church Composers: A Ten-Year Report." It contains a wealth of insight into the nature of ritual music and has important things to say about the musical/liturgical/pastoral judgment applied to the selection of liturgical music.

I also recommend to you the writings of authors far more knowledgeable and eloquent than I, such as the late, much-loved Rev. Eugene Walsh, to whom this book is dedicated; Rev. Lucien Deiss, CCSP; Mr. Ed Gutfreund; Rev. Virgil Funk; Rev. Aidan Kavanagh, OSB; Rev. John Melloh, SM; Mr. Gabe Huck; and Rev. Jake Empereur, SJ, whose articles frequently appear in the magazine *Modern Liturgy*.

Press on, then. I promise to try my best not to bore you. In turn, if you find this book particularly interesting, the concepts informative, and the evaluation technique useful (or for that matter, if you find it singularly vapid, devoid of intellectual content, and a waste of your time), won't you please take a moment to write down your thoughts and mail them to me at the following address:

Keith L. Patterson
c/o Resource Publications, Inc.
160 E. Virginia Street #290
San Jose, CA 95112-5876

I promise you a personal reply and my gratitude, for if an occasion ever arises to prepare a revision to this work, I shall surely consider each and every remark that anyone has taken the time to share with me.

In addition, I'm available to help you conduct this evaluation process. If you would like me to come to your community to present a workshop or help with the implementation of the process, write to me at the same address as above.

Enough with the commercials already. Let's get started.

Part One: THE STANDARDS

1. Principles for Measurement

LET'S LOOK AT some general principles that define the shape of the liturgical music program we should be striving to attain. These express what we will refer to as "The Standards" upon which this evaluation model is built. If you're going to ask the question, "How am I doing?" you first have to know the answer to, "In comparison to what?"

General Principles

There's a dynamic rhythm to the Mass. It's like a dance or symphony. The Mass attempts to reach the entire person and create a space where worshippers can become aware of God's presence in the community. It's not a time and place to isolate ourselves from everything we are but rather to acknowledge

The main question to ask is this: Does this piece of music and my performance of it serve the worship needs of this assembly?

and lift up all that makes us who we are. Life is not static, and neither is the liturgy.

Within the Mass there are moments when we are still, quietly reflecting. There are moments when we actively acknowledge one another's presence and celebrate God's indwelling there. We pray silently, then out loud. Sometimes we speak; sometimes we sing. We listen and talk; we stand and sit and kneel.

When we enter wholly into this rhythm, we open ourselves up to a more fully enveloping and rewarding worship experience. Instead of blandly punching a once-a-week ticket to membership in the Church, we can make the liturgical celebration an exciting and uplifting high point of our week—something we look forward to, anticipate, and appreciate. Our experience of the liturgy is enlivened when we discover and honor these rhythms.

There are two musical peaks in the Mass. The first occurs during the Liturgy of the Word with the gospel acclamation. The second occurs during the Liturgy of the Eucharist with the "core" acclamations ("Holy, Holy, Holy..."; memorial acclamation; and Great Amen). The eucharistic prayer is the universal prayer of the whole church, a magnificent and moving prayer that sums up our faith, our history, and our relationship with God as his people. It is at the Great Amen that we affirm our priesthood and affix our seal of approval to this prayer, accepting it and declaring it as our own with a resounding "*Amen!*" For a more detailed discussion of the rhythm of the liturgy, read *The Theology of Celebration* by Rev. Eugene Walsh (listed in the Bibliography).

Our liturgies are filled with words and symbols aimed at helping us enter into the worship experience more fully: prayers, banners, colors, incense, genuflections and other movements, silence, and music. All of these and more come together to help us enter into and lift up our communal prayer.

Principles Applying to Music in Liturgies

It is imperative that music *serve* the liturgy, not *dominate* it. Those involved with liturgical music must view themselves first as music *ministers*, then as *musicians*. Technical expertise and proficient performance simply aren't enough to make for good *liturgical* music. As a *musician*, I might want to sing a particular song next Sunday because it's a fine piece of music and I can perform it well. However, as a *minister*, I have to ask myself the following questions:

- Will this music enhance this liturgy?
- Will it help the assembly pray and celebrate?
- Will it fit in with the theme and feeling of the readings/homily of this day?
- Will it support the natural flow and rhythm of the liturgy, or conflict with it?
- Does the assembly know it? Will they sing it?

Sometimes, very competent musicians mistake "good" music for liturgically appropriate music. That is, just because a piece of music is well written and well performed doesn't mean it will minister to the worshipping community's needs in this place, at this time, in these circumstances. What might work well in a religious concert setting won't always work in a liturgical setting.

The main question to ask is this: Does *this* piece of music and my performance of it serve the worship needs of *this* assembly? The following section discusses what the guiding documents say and what guidelines to follow in determining what is "good" and "bad" in a given liturgical setting.

2. What the Guiding Documents Say

About Music in Liturgy

...*the liturgy is the summit* towards which the activity of the Church is directed; at the same time *it is the fount* from which all her power flows (The Constitution on the Sacred Liturgy [CSL], 10; emphasis added).

We are celebrating when we involve ourselves meaningfully in the thoughts, words, songs, and gestures of the worshipping community—when everything we do is wholehearted and authentic for us—when we mean the words and want to do what is done. *People in love make signs of love, not only to express their love but also to deepen it. Love never expressed dies. Christians' love for Christ and for each other, Christians' faith in Christ and in each other, must be expressed in the signs and symbols of celebration or it will die* (Music in Catholic Worship [MCW], 3-4; emphasis added).

Among the many signs and symbols used by the Church to celebrate its faith, *music is of preeminent importance.* ...the function of music is ministerial; it must serve and never dominate. Music should assist the assembled believers to express and share the gift of faith... It should heighten the texts so that they speak more fully and more effectively (MCW, 23; emphasis added).

...it should be recalled that *"liturgical worship is* given a *more noble* form when it is *celebrated with song..."* (General Instruction of the Roman Missal [GI], Foreword, 20; emphasis added).

The faithful who gather to await the Lord's coming are urged by the Apostle Paul to sing psalms, hymns and inspired songs (see Colossians 3:16). Song is the sign of the heart's joy (see Acts 2:46), and Saint Augustine said: "To sing belongs to lovers." Even in antiquity it was proverbial to say, "He prays twice who sings well." *Singing should be widely used* at Mass, depending on the type of people and the capability of each congregation, *but it is not always necessary to sing all the texts which were composed for singing. Preference should be given to the more significant parts, especially* those to be sung by the priest or ministers with the people responding or *those to be sung* by the priest and people *together* (GI, 19; emphasis added).

Increasingly, we are coming to understand how *a rite and* its sound, *its music, are inseparable:* serving, enabling and *revealing aspects of our belief that would otherwise remain unexpressed* ("The Milwaukee Symposia for Church Composers: A Ten-Year Report" [MSCC], 4; emphasis added).

Just as the inflection of human speech shapes the meaning of our words, so can *music open up new*

> *meanings in sung texts* as well as the liturgical unit that is the setting for such texts (MSCC, 15; emphasis added).
>
> Music has a natural *capacity to unite* the singer with the song, the singer with those who listen, singers with each other. Christian ritual song *joins the assembly with Christ*, who is the source and the content of the song. *The song of the assembly is an event of the presence of Christ* (MSCC, 16; emphasis added).

About Music Selection

The Threefold Judgment

Music in Catholic Worship cites a threefold judgment to be made in the evaluation of music in celebration. Although we frequently treat these as three separate judgments, they are really three aspects of a single judgment.

> One difficulty [with applying the criteria established by Music in Catholic Worship] is the tendency to treat the musical-liturgical-pastoral judgment as three separate judgments...[instead] of a single, multifaceted judgment for evaluating musical elements in worship (MSCC, 82).

The Musical Aspect

> *Is the music* technically, aesthetically and expressively *good?* This judgment...should be made by competent musicians...The musician has every right to insist that the music be good. But although all liturgical music should be good music, not all good music is suitable to the liturgy. The musical judgment is basic but not final. There remain the liturgical and pastoral judgments (MCW, 26-29; emphasis added).

The Liturgical Aspect

This judgment is based on two parts: structural requirements and textual requirements.

Structural Requirements

> The nature of the liturgy itself will help to determine what kind of music is called for, what parts are to be preferred for singing and who is to sing them. *The choice of sung parts, the balance* between them and the style of musical setting used *should reflect the relative importance* of the parts of the Mass...and the nature of each part. Thus elaborate settings of the entrance song, "Lord Have Mercy" and "Glory to God" may make the proclamation of the word seem unimportant; an overly elaborate offertory song with a spoken "Holy, Holy, Holy Lord" may make the eucharistic prayer seem less important (MCW, 30-31; emphasis added).

Textual Requirements

> *Does the music express...the text correctly and make it more meaningful?* ...[T]exts..."should be drawn chiefly from holy scripture and from liturgical sources" (MCW, 32; emphasis added).

The Pastoral Aspect

> Ideally this judgment is made by the planning team or committee. Does music in the celebration enable *these* people to express their faith, in *this* place, in *this* age, in *this* culture? (MCW, 39; emphasis added).

Music selection must acknowledge and honor the cultural and linguistic diversity that exists within the parish (see MSCC, 62). Defining a parish's constituency is an ongoing process—we are a mobile society; people come and go. What are the cultural, ethnic, and linguistic backgrounds of the members of your assembly, right now? Your answer today may be different than it would have been ten years ago.

When evaluating how well your music ministry teams have applied the musical-liturgical-pastoral judgment in their music selections, you must first know who is in the pews. To requote Music in Catholic Worship: "Does music in the celebration enable *these* people to express their faith, in *this* place, in *this* age, in *this* culture?" (MCW, 39; emphasis added).

Of all the contexts influencing this musical-liturgical-pastoral judgment, the cultural one is the most decisive (MSCC, 86).

Levels of Emphasis in the Mass

Overview

Integrity and unity in the rite suggest that the musical contour support the larger ritual units (MSCC, 43).

Proper preparation requires identification...and recognition of which [portions of the liturgy] are primary and which are secondary. A chronological preparatory process should be replaced by a process that takes the primary liturgical units as the starting point for the beginning and the center of the preparatory process (MSCC, 40).

Introductory Rites

The parts preceding the liturgy of the word, namely, the entrance, greeting, penitential rite, Kyrie, Gloria, and opening prayer...have the character of introduction and preparation. The purpose of these rites is to help the assembled...prepare...for listening to God's Word and celebrating the Eucharist. ...[T]he *entrance song and the opening prayer are primary.* All else is secondary (MCW, 44; emphasis added).

Liturgy of the Word

Readings from scripture are the heart of the liturgy of the word. The homily, responsorial psalms, profession of faith, and general intercessions develop and complete it...*[R]eadings, psalms, silence and the homily [are] of primary importance.* All else is secondary (MCW, 45; emphasis added).

Eucharistic Prayer

The eucharistic prayer...is the *center of the entire celebration.* [I]t is affirmed and ratified by...the... *Sanctus, the memorial acclamation and the Great Amen* (MCW, 47; emphasis added).

Communion Rite

The eating and drinking of the Body and Blood of the Lord in a paschal meal is the climax of our eucharistic celebration. [The primary parts] *are the Lord's Prayer, the song during the communion procession, and the prayer after communion* (MCW, 48; emphasis added).

Concluding Rite

The concluding rite consists of the priest's greeting and blessing...and the dismissal... *A recessional song is optional* (MCW, 49).

Repetition

> Because repetition is at the basis of all ritual and so of all ritual music, ...we need music that the community can begin to sing, even at its first hearing, with sufficient nuance and compositional richness that it can bear the weight of repetition and can continue to inspire the sung prayer of the assembly (MSCC, 21).

> The language of liturgical preparation implicitly acknowledges the repetitive nature of Christian ritual. This principle of repetition, however, can appear contrary to our culture, which often affirms that newer is better. Our preparation of the liturgy must respect...[t]he repetitive elements...[which]...create a ritual guarantee, which...allows the assembly to enter their rites fully (MSCC, 30).

On a broader scale, there should be a core repertoire that is repeated and shared among all the various services that occur at a parish each weekend.

> Often the "folk" group, the "adult" choir, the cantors and the organist minister at separate eucharists, each with its own repertoire. Not only does this inhibit the development of a core repertoire, but it has the potential to express and create divisions within a community at the very heart of its identity....One of those goals [for the musical leadership] will be forging a shared repertoire of acclamations, responses and other service music for all the Sunday assemblies....[T]his common repertoire can help to unify a local community, unavoidably divided by several Sunday eucharists (MSCC, 22).

Silence and Instrumental Music

> Silence should be observed at designated times... At the penitential rite and again after the invitation to pray, each one should become recollected (in silence); at the conclusion of a reading or the homily, each one meditates briefly on what he has heard; after communion, he praises God in his heart and prays (GI, 23).
>
> A more lengthy pause for reflection may take place at the penitential rite and after the readings or homily. *The proper use of periods of silent prayer and reflection will help to render the celebration less mechanical and impersonal and lend a more prayerful spirit to the liturgical rite. Just as there should be no celebration without song, so too there should be no celebration without periods for silent prayer and reflection* (GI, Foreword, 13; emphasis added).

The best places for instrumental music are "...prelude[s], a soft background to a spoken psalm, at the preparation of the gifts..., during portions of the communion rite, and the recessional" (MCW, 37).

Order of Importance among the Categories of Music

Acclamations are the most important category.

> *The acclamations are shouts of joy* which arise from the whole assembly as forceful and meaningful assents to God's Word and Action. They are important because they make some of the most significant moments of the Mass (gospel, eucharistic prayer, Lord's Prayer) stand out (MCW, 53; emphasis added).
>
> It is of their nature that they be *rhythmically strong, melodically appealing, and affirmative* (MCW, 53; emphasis added).
>
> [T]here are five acclamations which *ought to be sung even at Masses in which little else is sung*: Alleluia;

Acclamations are the most important category.

> "Holy, Holy, Holy Lord"; Memorial Acclamation; Great Amen; Doxology to the Lord's Prayer (MCW, 54; emphasis added).

The two categories of music next in importance are the entrance and communion *processionals* (MCW, 60-62) and the *responsorial psalm* (MCW, 63).

The *ordinary chants* should not overshadow the first three categories of music. These are: "Lord, Have Mercy"; "Glory to God"; Lord's Prayer; "Lamb of God"; and profession of faith (MCW, 64-69).

The final and least important category in terms of liturgical priority is the *supplementary songs*. They can consist of solos, choral pieces, instrumental or congregational pieces. It's important *not* to get locked into singing them all the time. These are: music during the preparation of the gifts; thanksgiving after communion; recessional; and litanies (MCW, 70-74).

About Each Singable Moment

Entrance

> The general instruction takes for granted that *there will be singing at the entrance* of the priest and other ministers... (GI, Foreword, 18; emphasis added).

> The *purpose* of this song is to *open* the celebration, *deepen the unity* of the people, *introduce* them *to the* mystery of the season or *feast*, and *accompany the [entrance] procession*. [It may be] sung alternately by the choir and people or by the cantor and the people; or it is sung entirely by the people or the choir alone (GI, 25-26; emphasis added).

> The entrance song should create an *atmosphere of celebration*. It serves the function of putting the assembly in the proper frame of mind for listening to the Word of God. It helps people to become conscious of themselves as a worshipping community. ...[D]uring the most important seasons of the Church year, Easter, Lent, Christmas and Advent, it is preferable that most songs used at the entrance be seasonal in nature (MCW, 61).

"Lord, Have Mercy"

> *When sung*, the setting should be brief and simple so as not to give undue importance to the introductory rites (MCW, 65; emphasis added).

From this I conclude that the Kyrie is not normally sung as a matter of course.

"Glory to God"

> The Gloria...[may be] sung by the congregation, by the people alternately with the choir, or by the choir alone. ...The Gloria is sung or said on Sundays *outside Advent and Lent*, on *solemnities and feasts...* (GI, 31; emphasis added).

> The *restricted use* of the Gloria, i.e., only on Sundays outside Advent and Lent and on solemnities and feasts, emphasizes its special and solemn character (MCW, 66; emphasis added).

Responsorial Psalm

> The cantor of the psalm sings the verse at the lectern or other suitable place, while the...congregation takes part by singing the response... (GI, 36)

> [The responsorial psalm] is the response to the first lesson. The new lectionary lists 900 refrains in its determination to match the content of the psalms to the theme of the reading. The liturgy of the Word comes to life if between the first two readings a cantor sings the psalm and all sing the response. Since most groups cannot learn a new response every week, seasonal refrains are offered in the lectionary itself and in the *Simple Gradual* (MCW, 63).

Use of seasonal responsorial psalm refrains is an excellent way to increase the assembly's participation in this moment. I highly recommend it.

Gospel Acclamation

> The alleluia...may be omitted if not sung (GI, 39).

> [The alleluia is] a preparation for the gospel. All stand to sing it...*If not sung, it may be omitted* (MCW, 55; emphasis added).

Profession of Faith

> If [the Creed] is sung, this is ordinarily done by the people together or in alternation (GI, 43-44; emphasis added).
>
> It is usually preferable that the Creed be spoken...rather than sung (MCW, 69).

General Intercessions

Only in passing does the General Instruction make mention of sung intercessions or responses (GI, 47). Music in Catholic Worship doesn't refer to music in connection with this liturgical moment at all. I conclude from this that it is not a normal practice to sing the intercessions, and, singing them should be reserved for occasional emphasis.

Preparation of the Gifts

> [It is preferred that there be] song or other music [to accompany] the preparation of the gifts (GI, Foreword, 14).
>
> The *procession with the gifts* is accompanied by the offertory song, which continues at least until the gifts are placed on the altar. The rules for the offertory song are the same as those for the entrance song... (GI, 50; emphasis added).
>
> The offertory song need not speak of bread and wine or of offering. The proper function of the offertory song is...to accompany...the procession [with the gifts].... [D]uring...Easter time, Lent, Christmas and Advent, it is preferable that most songs used during the offertory be seasonal in character. During the remainder of the Church year, however, topical songs may be used.... (GI, Appendix 1, 50).
>
> The [offertory] procession *can* be accompanied by song. *Song is not always necessary* or desirable. Organ or instrumental music is also fitting at this time....If there is no singing or organ or instrumental music, this may be a period of silence....*In fact, it is good to give the assembly a period of quiet* (that is, while the gifts are prepared and placed on the altar...).... (GI, Appendix 1, 50; emphasis added).
>
> The offertory song may accompany the procession and preparation of the gifts. *It is not always necessary or*

desirable. Organ or instrumental music is also fitting at the time. When song is used it is to be noted that the song need not speak of bread and wine or of offering. The proper function of this song is to accompany and celebrate the communal aspects of the procession. The text, therefore, can be any appropriate song of praise or of rejoicing in keeping with the season (MCW, 71; emphasis added).

"Core" Acclamations

The following three acclamations of the eucharistic prayer (the "Holy, Holy, Holy...," the memorial acclamation, and the Great Amen) should be in balance and harmony with one another.

The ideal is a unified and balanced use of the various musical elements within [each] liturgical unit. For example, LMT [Liturgical Music Today] recommends the employment of acclamations of a single, unified style throughout the eucharistic prayer (MSCC, 43).

"Holy, Holy, Holy..."

[T]he congregation sings or recites the Sanctus (GI, 55b; emphasis added).

Settings which add harmony or descants on solemn feasts and occasions are appropriate, but since this *chant* belongs to priest and people, the choir parts must facilitate and make effective the people's parts (MCW, 56; emphasis added).

Memorial Acclamation

This...is...a memorial of the Lord's suffering and glorification... (MCW, 57).

All should listen to the eucharistic prayer in silent reverence and share in it by making the acclamations (GI, 55h).

Great Amen

The worshippers *assent to the eucharistic prayer* and make it their own in the Great Amen. To be most effective, the Amen may be repeated or augmented. Choirs may harmonize and expand upon the people's acclamation (MCW, 58; emphasis added).

Lord's Prayer and Doxology

[T]he Lord's Prayer [is] sung or spoken aloud (GI, 56a).

"The [offertory] procession can be accompanied by song... If there is no singing or organ or instrumental music, this may be a period of silence... In fact, it is good to give the assembly a period of quiet..." (GI, Appendix 1, 50).

> [S]ettings must provide for the *participation of* the priest and *all present* (MCW, 67; emphasis added).

> [The doxology to the Lord's Prayer is] fittingly sung by all especially *when the Lord's Prayer is sung"* (MCW, 59; emphasis added).

The text of the Lord's Prayer belongs to the category of "ordinary chants," fourth in order of importance, and as such should not overshadow the first three categories of music—acclamations, processionals and responsorial psalm (see MCW, 64-69). In general, singing the Lord's Prayer should probably be saved for special occasions.

The Doxology at the end of the Lord's Prayer ("For the Kingdom, the power and the glory...") falls into the category of "acclamation" (first in order of importance) and should normally be sung. Speaking the Lord's Prayer and singing the Doxology may feel a bit awkward at first; once you've tried it a few times, however, you'll find that the rhythm of it is quite pleasing.

One more consideration with regard to singing the Lord's Prayer is that settings must be very simple and well known—otherwise, the people won't be able to fully participate and will be robbed of their rightful role in this liturgical moment.

"Lamb of God"

> [D]uring the breaking of the bread...the Agnus Dei is ordinarily sung by the choir or cantor with the people responding; or it may be said aloud (GI, 56e).

The length of the singing should roughly match the amount of time it takes to complete the fraction rite.

> [The Lamb of God] is...to accompany the breaking of the bread...It may be sung by the choir [alone], though the people should generally make the response (MCW, 68).

Communion

> The general instruction takes for granted that there will be singing...(...at the communion rite...)... (GI, Foreword, 18).

> [T]he general instruction call[s] for singing during...communion...to "express the union of the communicants who join their voices in a single song,

"The communion song should foster a sense of unity. It should be simple and not demand great effort" (MCW, 62).

show the joy of all, and make the communion procession an act of brotherhood" (GI, Foreword, 19).

The Communion song should foster a sense of unity. It should be simple and not demand great effort. It gives expression to the joy of unity in the body of Christ.... Most benediction hymns...are not acceptable.... [D]uring...Easter time, Lent, Christmas and Advent, it is preferable that most songs used at the Communion be seasonal in nature. During the remainder of the Church year...topical songs may be used.... (GI, Appendix 1, 56i; MCW, 62).

Thanksgiving after Communion

After communion, the priest and people may spend some time in prayer. If desired, a hymn, psalm, or other song of praise *may* be sung... (GI, Foreword, 15; emphasis added).

After communion, the priest and people may spend some time in *silent prayer. If desired*, a hymn, psalm, or other *song* of praise *may be sung* by the entire congregation (GI, 56j; emphasis added).

From this I conclude that silence is preferable.

Recessional

The recession *may* be accompanied by song or other music (GI, Foreword, 17; emphasis added).

The General Instruction makes no reference to a recessional hymn or song within its discussion of the concluding rite. I conclude that it is of low importance in comparison with the other sung parts.

The recessional song has never been an official part of the rite; hence musicians are free to plan music which provides an appropriate closing to the liturgy. A song is one possible choice. However, if the people have sung a song after communion, it may be advisable to use only an instrumental or choir recessional (MCW, 73).

Summary

I trust that the foregoing discussion has sufficiently emphasized the need to acknowledge and honor the "ebb and flow" of the liturgical experience in our selection and presentation of ritual music.

The Liturgical Music Emphasis Chart on the facing page summarizes what the guiding liturgical music documents have to say about the relative emphasis of each of the singable moments within the liturgy.

The General Instruction discusses each of the parts of the Mass (i.e., introductory rites, Liturgy of the Word, etc.) and tells us which ones are more important to the liturgical action. The GI "weights" are indicated in the column marked "GI". The term "primary" indicates the part's great importance to the structure of the Mass. "Secondary" indicates less importance. "NR" stands for "Not Rated" and indicates that the GI did not specifically "rate" that portion and (therefore is of least importance musically).

The Music in Catholic Worship (MCW) "Weight" column mirrors the categories above but applies them to each of the singable moments within each part of the Mass.

The MCW "Ratings" were derived from the stated or implied level of emphasis contained within the text of the document. These fall into six categories as follows:

1 - Must always be sung by everyone.

2 - Should be sung by everyone. Antiphonally with choir/cantor OK.

3 - Should usually be sung. Antiphonal arrangement preferred.

4 - Reserve for special occasions or practical reasons (e.g., extended fraction rite).

5 - Prefer silence, spoken word or instrumental over singing.

NR - A rating couldn't be determined from the MCW discussion.

Liturgical Music Emphasis Chart

Part	GI Weight	MCW Weight	MCW Rating	Notes
Prelude	NR	NR	NR	If used, prefer instrumental.
Practice	NR	NR	NR	Depends on assembly and occasion.[1]
Entrance	Secondary	Primary	2	Based on readings or seasonal (preferred).
"Lord, Have Mercy"/ Sprinkling	Secondary	Secondary	4	*When* sung, do antiphonally; simple settings.
"Glory to God"	Secondary	Secondary	4	Reserve for special occasions.
Responsorial Psalm	Primary	Primary	3	Do antiphonally; seasonal setting OK.
Gospel Acclamation	Primary	Primary	1	Must sing.
Profession of Faith	Primary	Secondary	4	Usually spoken.
General Intercessions	Primary	Secondary	5	Usually spoken.
Preparation of the Gifts	Primary	Secondary	5	Prefer silence, instrumental, or quiet music.
"Holy, Holy, Holy..."	Primary	Primary	1	Should sing.
Memorial Acclamation	Primary	Primary	1	Should sing; add harmonies.
Great Amen	Primary	Primary	1	Should sing; add harmonies and repetitions.
Lord's Prayer	Primary	Primary	4	Usually spoken.
Doxology	Primary	Primary	1	Generally sung.
"Lamb of God"	Primary	Secondary	4	If fraction rite is extended (the norm), sing it. Otherwise it is spoken.
Communion	Primary	Primary	2	Based on readings or seasonal (preferred).
Thanksgiving after Communion	Secondary	Secondary	5	Silence is preferred.
Recessional	Secondary	Secondary	5	Singing not required. Instrumental and choral works OK.
Postlude	NR	NR	NR	

1 If a singing congregation is the norm, and the songs to be used are well known, a prelude may be used to set the "mood" for the celebration. If some music is unfamiliar *or* if the congregation is known to be a non-singing assembly (or their singing participation level is not known), then a practice is preferred.

Part Two:
THE EVALUATION MODEL

3. Pre-Survey Preparation

THE FIRST STEP is to choose a Coordinator to lead the evaluation and set a date for conducting the survey. He or she should be familiar with the principles of good liturgical music (found in Part One) and become thoroughly acquainted with this handbook. The most logical choice is the music director, but anyone with a working knowledge of liturgy can fill the bill.

Introduce the Coordinator to the liturgy committee and musicians. Let them know that the evaluation is going to take place, when it will happen, and who will be running it.

A word of caution: That part of the liturgical music program which has to do with "making music" poses a unique problem that must be taken into account from the outset. Many musicians are touchy about being "evaluated." There is, of necessity, a certain amount of ego involvement in the creative process of making music. When you tell musicians that their performance is going to be evaluated, you may raise a lot of insecurities and receive much resistance. It is critical to the success of this undertaking that you reassure them that the purpose of the evaluation is to help everyone take an objective look at the entire program and to discuss *together* what (and whether) any changes are needed. The purpose is not to point fingers or embarrass anyone.

I recommend the Coordinator conduct a seminar for the music ministers to explain the process and review the criteria that will be used to evaluate the program. The training need not be in-depth. Reading and discussing the Standards should suffice. Emphasize that the Standards presented in Part One are not arbitrary rules slapped together by the Coordinator, the pastor, the liturgy committee, or this author, but rather a summary of what the teaching authority of the Church has to say about the place of music in our worship services. I recommend that you conduct the workshop a couple of weeks prior to performing the evaluation.

What follows is a Pre-Survey Training Session Plan. I have found it to work quite well, but you may modify it to meet the needs of your specific group of musicians.

Pre-Survey Training Session Plan

Preparation

One Month Prior to Training

When you set up your Pre-Survey Training Session (which should be one to two weeks prior to the date established for the survey), work with parish councils, liturgy committees, and so on to ensure that the training will not conflict with any other scheduled activity. Arrange for an adequate space given the number of attendees you expect, etc. Here are some considerations for planning your meeting place:

- The environment should be friendly: no distracting outside noises and activities, reasonable temperature and air circulation, comfortable chairs, good lighting, access to restrooms, etc. Additionally, if you have handicapped or challenged members in your music groups, make sure the facility is accessible to them (accessible by a wheelchair ramp, elevator, etc.).

- Writing surfaces should be available. Chairs set up around tables is ideal.

- The ability to "break out" into smaller groups is important to the success of this training session. Some portions call for everyone to be together; other portions call for the participants to work in smaller groups. One large gathering space with smaller break-out rooms is ideal, but movable tables and chairs work, too.

- Since the training session is approximately eight hours in length, you'll want to give some consideration to eating arrangements. Do you want the participants to "brown bag it" or bring a potluck dish? Whatever you decide, make sure that the training space has appropriate accommodations (i.e., space for eating sack lunches, kitchen facilities for warming food, etc.).

- If there are many young parents in your music groups, you may want to make babysitting arrangements. Put yourself in the shoes of your liturgical musicians. Who are they? What are their needs? The more you can anticipate these and other concerns, the more you can plan accommodations. When you plan accommodations to meet their needs, you increase their interest and willingness to attend.

- Will you need a microphone or lectern? What will the musicians need to lead the singing—piano, music stand, etc.? Consider these elements as well when you plan where to have your training session.

Three Weeks Prior to Training

The Coordinator (or whoever will be the "instructor" for this training session) should *personally* contact the leaders of *every* music group that will be invited to take part in the training session. Phone calls are OK, but face-to-face discussion is more effective and inviting.

Communicate to the group leaders that *everyone* in the group is *strongly* encouraged to attend because they will be learning important skills that will make them more effective music ministers. Emphasize that this is a *self*-evaluation tool designed to give each group their own feedback about what kind of job they're doing.

This is a good time to take care of several other details as well.

- Determine if the pastor will be present, at least for the beginning of the training session. I recommend it; a display of pastoral support is a strong psychological tool for "gathering" the participants and focusing them while emphasizing the importance of the training. Acknowledging that pastors are stretched very thin these days, his presence isn't necessary for the entire session, just the introductory part.

- Determine who will lead and accompany the singing (there's a gathering and a closing song). Find out what they will need (piano, amplification, music stand, etc.).

Two Weeks Prior to Training

The parish should mail an announcement to the home of *every* liturgical musician, inviting them once again to attend. Re-emphasize that everyone in the group is strongly encouraged to participate and that the survey process is a *self*-evaluation tool. I recommend that the pastor sign the letter—it generally carries more weight that way.

Besides "selling" the fact that this is an opportunity for members to understand their ministry more deeply, make sure to cover the logistics, such as where the training will be, when, and what to bring (lunch, etc.). Be sure to include a phone number for a point of contact in case they have questions (I recommend you use the Coordinator's home phone number.)

One Week Prior to Training

Make sure to print a reminder in the church bulletin and include an announcement at each Mass.

Several days before the training, call *every* liturgical musician and restate your personal invitation to attend the training session. The Coordinator should have some help with the calling. Perhaps you can work with the leaders of each group, or a small committee of helpers can assist. Making phone calls may seem like a hassle, but this little gesture of personal contact really pays high dividends in terms of attendance.

During your phone conversation, determine if the person will be attending. If not, find out why and see if you can help them overcome whatever would keep him or her away. For instance, if the person needs transportation, see if someone else can carpool with him or her. If the person has small children and can't get away, see if someone can help out with babysitting. Just be honest and warm and hospitable. Your good attitude will be attractive and will encourage a higher level of participation.

Make sufficient copies of each of the four evaluation forms, plus all of Part One of this book to ensure that every attendee at the training session will have a personal copy to work from. Make a few extras in case someone you didn't expect shows up. It's better to have too many copies than too few—you can always use the extras for another training session. Make enough copies of the *entire* Evaluation Form 1 package (including instructions) to supply between three and five evaluators for each service.

Have a supply of pencils and blank paper on hand. Make sure you have whatever resources you need for the singing: hymnals, songsheets (with reprint permission, of course!), and so on.

One Day Prior to Training

The Coordinator should make contact with those people who will assist with the training (accompanist, pastor, etc.). Make sure everyone knows where they're supposed to be and when, and what they'll be doing.

The Training Session

The Coordinator should arrive *at least* one half hour before the participants and accomplish the following last-minute preparations:

- Check out the environment (light, temperature, etc.).
- Set up the training area (chairs, tables, lectern, microphone, etc.).
- Place the handouts, pencils, and other supplies near the door with a sign for attendees to pick up materials as they enter. (Note: Do not set the materials out ahead of time on the chairs or tables. There's a subtle reason for this. If you set out all the materials before people arrive and then only fill half of the chairs, participants will have an initial impression like, "I wonder where everyone else is. What do they know that I don't?" That's not a good way to start out a training session. If participants pick up materials *as they come in*, you won't have that problem. Likewise, you should direct people where to sit when they come in. Fill up available seating from front to back. These are small details, but they help with first impressions and that's important in any training session.)

Introduction

Step 1 *(5 minutes)*

When everyone has arrived and you're ready to begin, the Coordinator should cue the musician(s) to begin the gathering song. Don't try to out-yell the attendees or wave them into their seats. Just start the song—that'll focus and gather them.

Choose a song that focuses on service or ministry—one that they're very familiar with and can join in spontaneously. Perhaps "Service" (Ceasar), "Here I Am" (Schutte), "Servant Song" (McGargill), or "In Christ There Is No East or West" (Oxenham).

I recommend that you sing whatever song you've chosen in its entirety. *Enjoy* the song. *Pray* the song. Encourage the participants to add harmony. They are musicians, after all—let them use their gifts.

Step 2 *(5 minutes)*

Immediately after the song, while everyone is still standing, the pastor should lead a short prayer along the lines of "Thanks for the gift of music" and "Help us to become more faithful servants," etc.

He then invites everyone to be seated, introduces the Coordinator, and indicates that this individual has his full support and that the evaluation process will help the music ministers do an even better job of praising God through music.

Step 3 *(5 minutes)*

If the Coordinator is going to teach the session, launch immediately into the next step. If someone else will perform the training, the Coordinator introduces the Instructor with a few words about his or her background, etc.

Step 4 *(15 minutes)*

If there are attendees present who do not know one another, briefly go around the room and have the participants introduce themselves, stating at least their name, which group they are associated with, and what role they play (e.g., sing, accompany, etc.).

Step 5 *(5 minutes)*

Begin with a brief discussion of music ministry. Explain that as liturgical musicians, we are concerned with not only how *good* the music is but how well it helps the assembly experience the presence of God. Explain that the Church has provided guidance for music ministers in The Constitution on the Sacred Liturgy, The General Instruction of the Roman Missal, Music in Catholic Worship, and Liturgical Music Today (display copies of these if available).

Step 6 *(5 minutes)*

Indicate that a summary of the guidance provided in the documents is contained in the handout (Part One of this book) they picked up as they entered. State that the purpose of today's training session is to explore the Standards in those documents and that each of the music groups will discuss *among themselves* how these Standards apply to their ministry.

Focus on the evaluation process as a self-improvement tool. Point out that this is an opportunity to step back, take a look at what they've been doing, acknowledge what has worked well, and plan how to make their ministries more effective, powerful and prayerful.

Step 7 *(5 minutes)*

Indicate that within the next couple of weeks each group will be evaluating their own ministry in light of these Standards and determining what (if any) changes to make. Announce the dates on which the evaluations will take place. Indicate that at the end of the training session today, the Coordinator will be looking for volunteers to help with the evaluation process. Indicate that there will be more about this later in the training.

Step 8 *(10 minutes)*

Announce a break and give attendees an opportunity to get coffee, socialize a bit, etc.

Review of Guiding Documents

Step 9 *(5 minutes)*

Reconvene the session. Ensure that everyone has a copy of Part One, "The Standards," and something to write with.

Step 10 *(10 minutes)*

Begin with the General Principles and Principles Applying to Music in Liturgies in Chapter 1. These two sections should be read aloud in their entirety. The reading may be accomplished in any way you prefer. However, I recommend that you call on volunteers to read individual paragraphs. Those who read out loud will be more focused on the content. Using a variety of resources will interest and hold your participants' attention.

Step 11 *(5 minutes)*

Pause to see if there are any questions thus far. Briefly re-emphasize that there is a rhythm to the Mass and the music needs to "go with the flow," not conflict with it.

Step 12 *(5 minutes)*

Move on to Chapter 2, "What the Guiding Documents Say." Invite one person to read the first section, About Music in Liturgy. The Instructor is the preferable reader, but anybody with a good speaking voice may read this out loud.

The reader should pause in between the eight quotes. Instead of waiting until you reach the end of each paragraph to identify which document it comes from, I recommend that you begin each paragraph by saying something like, "The Constitution on the Sacred Liturgy says that...," then continue with the quote. No discussion is necessary; just let the attendees hear and think about each quote.

Ask everyone to mark these pages and refer to them from time to time as a focal point of reference.

Step 13 *(10 minutes)*

Invite the attendees to read the next section, About Music Selection, to themselves. Let them know that there will be a discussion about this section afterward. Indicate that they have ten minutes to complete their reading. (Note: This is everything from the Threefold Judgment through Order of Importance among the Categories of Music, pages 13-18.)

Watch the attendees to see if they finish the reading early. If so, proceed to the discussion-generating questions below. If it looks like they will need more than ten minutes, encourage them to speed up, reminding them that the handouts are theirs to keep so they'll have a chance to read them in more detail later.

Step 14 *(15 minutes)*

When everyone is done reading, ask the following or similar questions. Don't provide the answers; pose the questions and let the attendees come up with the answers. Give them time to discuss varying opinions. If you get anxious about the amount of time this is taking, you can either cut out some of the questions and encourage the attendees to review those sections in detail later, or let the discussion continue and shorten something else later on.

- What is the Threefold Judgment?

- What do you think is the most important or interesting aspect of the musical criteria?
- What do you think is the most important or interesting aspect of the liturgical criteria?
- What do you think is the most important or interesting aspect of the pastoral criteria?
- Not all parts of the Mass are equally emphasized. What are the two most important parts of the Mass?
- What is the most emphasized part of the Liturgy of the Word?
- What is the most emphasized part of the Liturgy of the Eucharist?
- What do the guiding documents say about silence? Why do you think silence is discussed in a book about liturgical music?
- What is the most important category of music at Mass?
- What is the least important category of music at Mass?

Step 15 *(5 minutes)*

Announce that they will cover the next section in small groups, and proceed with these instructions.

Once assembled, each group is to first select a spokesperson for their group, who will take notes and share the results of their group's discussion with the larger group at the end of the exercise. Tell them they will have two minutes to choose their spokesperson and thirteen minutes to discuss the item you'll assign them.

Divide the attendees into smaller discussion groups of *at least* three people and no more than seven. Do this by any method that works for you. You may prefer to let the attendees divide themselves up on their own. Or you may have everyone count off by threes, then all the "ones" form a group, the "twos" form another, and so on.

Once the groups are formed, assign one or more portions of the next section, About Each Singable Moment, to each group. Do not assign the Summary; you will cover that at the end.

Step 16 *(15 minutes)*

Direct the groups to their meeting places, whether in break-out rooms or in corners of the larger room, etc. Attendees move immediately into their discussion areas and set about choosing their spokesperson. Once that's done, they read their assigned section(s) and discuss. Their objective is to cover their assignment and be prepared to present a brief summary of the guidelines for each singable moment (e.g., entrance song; responsorial psalm; "Holy, Holy, Holy..."; etc.).

Step 17 *(15 minutes)*

Call for a break. Groups may continue to discuss if they've not finished yet. At the end of the break, everyone should convene in the large group once again.

Step 18 *(45 minutes)*

Reconvene the session and invite each group's spokesperson to share the results of their discussion, focusing on what the group found to be most important, interesting or surprising. I recommend that you call on the spokespersons according to the order of the topics in the section, About Each Singable Moment. Ask the speakers to try to hold their comments to two or three minutes each.

When everyone has made their presentation, open the floor for discussion. It is *imperative* that everyone understand the concepts presented here because these are the foundation upon which the entire evaluation system is based. If you need more than forty-five minutes to make the presentations and hold discussion, take whatever time you need. Do not brush over this portion of training.

When the discussion are done, cover the Summary, focusing on the descriptions of the ratings categories.

Have everyone turn to the Liturgical Music Emphasis Chart, or project one onto a screen if an overhead and that manner of presentation is preferred. Give everyone an opportunity to look at the chart for a couple of minutes. Let them see the "big picture" of the relationship between all the sung parts of the Mass.

Instruct them that this chart summarizes what the guiding documents say about each singable moment and its relationship to the others. State that if our liturgical music is to minister most effectively within the context of the Mass, then what we sing and how we sing it should honor and enhance the natural rhythm of the Mass, not conflict with it. This chart makes it easier to determine what should be sung and when.

Read through each singable moment, calling attention especially to those items that have a rating of 1 or 2 in the Music in Catholic Worship rating column. Read the Notes out loud.

When you have reviewed the entire chart, indicate that the evaluation process will measure how well the music ministries apply these principles to the selection and execution of liturgical music. Suggest that those who plan the music should keep this chart handy when making their selections.

Let them know that each liturgical music ministry group will discuss among themselves what this chart and the information it represents means to them and their liturgical music program. Assure them that there will be many opportunities throughout the remainder of the training session to continue discussion on this topic, since it is the foundation of the evaluation process. If anything on the chart is unclear, open up the floor for discussion. This will allow you to clarify certain points, and everybody can "talk from the same book" for the rest of the session.

Note: It is likely that there will be some disagreement about the levels of emphasis—especially when the attendees read the Notes, which indicate what should and should not be sung. Give them time to talk through their differences. In each instance, look back with them to what the guiding documents say (Chapters 1 and 2) about what should and should not be emphasized. Further, point out that these are only guidelines, principles, and standards. The purpose of the guidelines is not to restrict and dictate and limit; rather the purpose is to help liturgical musicians make more effective choices. Such choices will reinforce the natural rhythm and flow of the liturgy, enhance the worship experience, and help to make God's presence more fully felt.

Step 19 *(60 minutes)*

Conclude the review of the guidelines and announce the break for a meal. Give the attendees an hour, indicating at what time they should reconvene.

Discussion of the Impact

Step 20 *(5 minutes)*

Reconvene the session. The easiest way to do this is to cue the musicians to sing another song. Either repeat what you sang for the gathering song or pick another appropriate, well-known song.

Step 21 *(15 minutes)*

Hand out to each participant the Pre-Survey Group Member Worksheet, "How Are We Doing?" Briefly review the forms (which are self-explanatory), then give them ten minutes to fill one out for the group of which they are a member. If they are a member of more than one group, direct them to fill out a form for one group only.

Let them know they will keep their own forms; that is, they won't be turned in to anyone. Their responses will be used during group discussions later.

Step 22 *(60 minutes)*

When everyone has finished filling out their forms, indicate that each group will get together and discuss what (if any) impact this information has on their choice or presentation of liturgical music. Specify where each group will meet. (Note: To reduce noise, it's best if each group can have their own room; however, if that's not practical, arrange the groups to allow for the greatest distance possible between them.)

Indicate that each group leader will direct a discussion of their current practices in light of the information presented at this training session. Do the members believe they are already making liturgically appropriate choices, or are some changes in order? Suggest they take their individual "How Are We Doing" worksheets to help in their discussion.

Hand out the Pre-Survey Group Leader Summary Sheet to each of the group leaders, indicating that they can use these to summarize their group's discussion. When the large group meets again, the group leaders will form a panel to offer conclusions and summaries.

Send the attendees off to their group discussions. Let them know they have approximately one hour to review and discuss before reconvening.

Circulate among the groups, making sure the discussion stays on the topic of how today's information has impacted their group. See that the leader is noting the discussion on the Summary sheet.

Step 23 *(15 minutes)*

Allow the groups a break. During the break, set up several chairs in front of the training area to accommodate a discussion panel that will consist of each of the group leaders.

Step 24 *(30 minutes)*

Reconvene the attendees in the general gathering area. Invite the leaders to come forward to take part in the panel discussion. Encourage the leaders to present those aspects of their group's discussion that seemed the most interesting, productive, or problematic. The point is to get them to share a little of what went on in each group. You might pose the following questions:

- What is the most useful or interesting information your group got out of this discussion?
- What is the item that generated the most discussion, and why?
- Are your group members generally satisfied with the "way things are," or do they want to make changes? If they want to make changes, what are they and why?

Make sure you give each group plenty of opportunity to talk, but don't let this drag on. When the conversation dies down, it's time to move on to closure.

When the leaders seem like they're "talked out," open the floor to other comments and questions from the rest of the attendees. Wing it; you can either answer the questions yourself or refer them to the panel. Make sure people have talked through what's on their minds before moving on.

When everyone is done, terminate the panel discussion and direct the leaders back to the general seating area.

Step 25 *(5 minutes)*

Summarize what has been accomplished so far. Cover at least the following:

- We explored what the guiding documents have to say about the rhythm and flow of the Mass and how music fits into that.
- We looked at some standards we can use when selecting liturgical music.
- We had a chance to discuss changes we'd like to make within our own programs.
- Our next step will be to conduct a full-fledged evaluation.

Step 26 *(15 minutes)*

Explain the evaluation process and indicate when it will take place.

Introduce the four evaluation forms, explaining that each one evokes responses from different points of view of their ministry.

Explain that Form 1 will be filled out by them—the liturgical music ministers. Each group will select their own evaluators. The evaluators can be from their own group or groups can exchange evaluators. Leave it up to each group to decide. Tell the attendees that after a general discussion of the evaluation process, each music ministry team will meet separately to discuss how they want to accomplish this part of the evaluation and get names of members to fill out the evaluation forms. Assure them that evaluators will receive detailed instructions for filling out the form—that it's pretty simple and straightforward and based on the material covered during the training session today.

Explain that Form 2 will be filled out by members of the liturgy committee. (Note: Make sure that this is the arrangement. It's what I recommend, but local circumstances may necessitate the enlistment of other evaluators. Just be sure to let your musicians know who is going to be evaluating them.)

Explain that Form 3 will be filled out by several people picked at random from the assembly.

Explain that Form 4 will be filled out by each group week by week over the coming year to track choices and patterns that extend over an entire season or liturgical year. The use of this form will be discussed in more detail during the Post-Survey Feedback Session.

Explain that all the completed forms will be turned over to each group, and that a Post-Survey Feedback Session will be held to review the results and discuss what they mean with respect to any changes the groups may wish to make to their programs.

Step 27 *(5 minutes)*

Direct the group's attention to their copies of Liturgical Music Ministry Evaluation Form 1. Explain that evaluators will fill this form out while the Mass is underway. They cannot take part in the music ministry while they are evaluating; they need to be out with the rest of the assembly. They should be familiar enough with the form that they can use it without being a distraction to those around them.

Note that Side One is basically a repeat of the Liturgical Music Emphasis Chart; that is, it measures how closely the group's choices of what to sing match up with the Standards expressed in the guiding documents. Side Two evaluates the presentation of the music—the accompanists, the cantors, etc. It also records the assembly's response to the music.

Point out that Forms 2 and 3 will be filled out by other people. Copies are provided here so they can see the types of things the other evaluators will be looking at. Copies of Form 4 will be retained by each group to record selections over the coming year. Explain that you will use Form 4 next year to study the quality of their liturgical music choices on a seasonal level. For example, it will help track choices such as:

- Do we choose Mass settings reflective of the mood of the liturgical season?
- Do we strive for a stronger, more participative repertoire by repeated use of quality music over a season or other period of time (vice changing all hymn selections every week)?

Step 28 *(15 minutes)*

Send the groups back into their own discussion areas to decide who will perform the evaluation for them. Point out that at least three to five people should evaluate each service.

Instruct group leaders to determine with their groups who is willing to be an evaluator (either for their own group or another). Each group will also decide if they want to do their own evaluation or exchange evaluators with another group.

Remind them that since the evaluators cannot take part in the music ministry on the week they perform the evaluation, they may have to plan around the loss of that person for that service. Alternatively, they can work out an arrangement with another group to exchange evaluators. That way, no one needs to miss participating in their own ministry. For example, a member of a group that provides music at a 10 o'clock service can stay and perform an evaluation for the 12 o'clock group. Likewise, someone from the 12 o'clock group can come early and evaluate the 10 o'clock service.

Let each music ministry team discuss this among themselves and then with the other groups. Let this discussion continue until each group has identified who will evaluate their service.

Step 29 *(10 minutes)*

When the discussion winds down and the decisions have been made, reconvene the general group. Go around the room and find out who will evaluate each service. Write down the names, continuing until all the services are covered. If any groups have not yet reached consensus, you can help facilitate those decisions at this point. When you are satisfied that every group has at least three to five evaluators, begin closure.

Step 30 *(5 minutes)*

Indicate that at the end of the session, all the evaluators will come forward to pick up their evaluation packages. Point out where they are and state that they include additional forms plus all the instructions.

Summarize the day's experience. If you have the ability to ad lib, recall any "in jokes" from the day's session (humorous occurrences, lively discussions, etc.). Express confidence that this training combined with the upcoming evaluation process will help to improve the quality of their liturgical music ministry.

If the session has been led by an Instructor, return control of the session to the Coordinator.

Step 31 *(10 minutes)*

If applicable, the Coordinator thanks the Instructor for his or her work. Thank the participants for taking the time to be part of the training and part of the process of improvement. If other thanks are in order (for food, facilities, whatever), make them now.

Close with a brief prayer of thanksgiving and an upbeat song such as "Glory and Praise" (Schutte), "Canticle of the Sun" (Haugen), "For the Beauty of the Earth" (Dix/Pierpoint), "Joyful, Joyful, We Adore Thee" (Van Dyke/Beethoven), or "Sing to the Mountains" (Dufford).

Terminate the session and invite the evaluators forward to pick up their packages (i.e., Appendix C).

4. Conducting the Survey

BEFORE HOLDING THE Pre-Survey Training Session, the Coordinator should become thoroughly familiar with the four evaluation forms (found in the Appendices) used in the evaluation process. "Why *four* forms?" you may ask. Each form accomplishes a separate purpose and is filled out by different individuals to bring a broader perspective to bear on the subject. Let's take a look at those forms.

How to Use the Forms

Complete Forms 1 through 3 on the same day. The process yields less-useful information if Form 1 is filled out one week, Form 2 another week, and so on. Completing Forms 1 through 3 all on the same day provides a much better snapshot of "the way we were" on *that* day, in *that* place, at *that* time.

Complete Forms 1 through 3 on the same day.

Form 4 has a slightly different focus and is not used as part of the initial evaluation cycle. Instead it is designed to be used over the course of an entire liturgical year and will become part of the annual follow-up evaluation cycle (see Chapter 6).

Evaluation Form 1: For Music Ministers

Evaluation Form 1, found in Appendix C, focuses on the process of selecting liturgically appropriate music and contains the most specific and invaluable information to be gathered from this process. Commensurately, it requires the most training to fill out properly. The training is accomplished during the Pre-Survey Training Session. All the necessary additional information is contained in the form's instructions, which were handed out during the training.

Selection of Evaluators

I recommend that you use music ministers to complete this evaluation form for the following reasons:

- It lowers resistance to the evaluation process itself since they will be evaluating their own work; there won't be an outsider "passing judgment" on them.
- They are more likely to believe in the results of the evaluation and take action on the recommendations when they are generated by members of their own group rather than by "outsiders."
- The evaluators will have to familiarize themselves with the Standards upon which the form is based; that will serve as an educational tool to make them more aware of the principles that should guide selection and presentation of liturgical music.

I recommend you use more than one evaluator for each service; their combined observations will have more credibility than any one person's. Using an odd number of evaluators (preferably three to five) helps to avoid "ties" in the evaluation results. This is purely a psychological ploy, but a helpful one. When evaluators are evenly split on an evaluation point, subsequent review and discussion of the results tends to focus just on those elements to the detriment of all the other factors that may be more clearly in need of attention and "fixing." I can't explain

If a group is too small to afford members to evaluate their own performance, coordinate evaluations between various music groups at your church or among several churches in the area.

the "why" of this dynamic; I can only share with you that I've seen it in action in post-survey group discussions time after time.

If a group is too small to afford members to evaluate their own performance, coordinate evaluations between various music groups at your church or among several churches in the area: "We'll visit and evaluate your services this week if you'll come over and evaluate ours the next."

It's best if the groups to be evaluated know ahead of time when it will take place. Some music directors maintain that it's better to spring the evaluation unannounced or perform it clandestinely so they can "catch them like they really are." They're concerned that, "If you tell them ahead of time, they might do a really good job on that day, then slip back into sloppy habits right afterward." I disagree. If a group can shine on an evaluation day, they can shine all the time. I believe that music ministers *want* to do a good job *all* the time, not just when they're being scrutinized. The process of *preparing* for the evaluation is just as instructive as the evaluation itself.

Reporting Results

If there were several evaluators, they should discuss their observations immediately after performing the evaluation, while the experience is still fresh in their minds. They should then turn in their evaluation forms to the Coordinator in person and discuss any items they feel need clarification or expansion.

The Coordinator should present the evaluators' findings to the group(s) evaluated as soon as possible. The section devoted to the Post-Survey Feedback fully explains this step.

Everyone has a bad day from time to time. Keep in mind that this process only provides a snapshot of how these evaluators perceived the music on this one particular day. You may wish to repeat the process a couple of times at first, say about one month apart. That will give a more accurate picture of the state of your liturgical music at a given service.

Repeat the process annually to measure improvement. Chapter 6, "Annual Follow-Up," will give you ideas for continuing the process on a year-to-year basis.

Evaluation Form 2: For Liturgy Committee Members

Evaluation Form 2, found in Appendix D, focuses on the ministerial aspect of the music program.

Selection of Evaluators

This form is designed to be filled out by a liturgically informed individual, but one who is preferably *not* involved with the music ministry. A liturgy committee member is an ideal choice. Solicit volunteers to fill out Form 2; again, three to five evaluators will be better than one.

No training is required. If the evaluator is already familiar with the concept of "ministry" and has a working knowledge of the principles of good liturgy, the only preparation he/she will need is to read the instructions on the evaluation sheet beforehand.

Evaluators should "sit out" when they perform the evaluation rather than take part in any other ministry.

Reporting Results

If there were several evaluators, they should discuss their observations immediately after performing the evaluation, while the experience is still fresh in their minds. They should then turn in their evaluation forms to the Coordinator in person and discuss any items they feel need clarification or expansion.

The Coordinator should present the evaluators' findings to the group(s) evaluated as soon as possible. The section devoted to the Post-Survey Feedback fully explains this step.

Keep in mind that this process only provides a snapshot of how these evaluators perceived the music on this one particular day. Repeat the process a couple of times at first, say about one month apart. That will give a more accurate picture of the state of your liturgical music at a given service.

As with Evaluation Form 1, repeat the use of Form 2 annually.

Evaluation Form 3: For the Assembly

Evaluation Form 3, found in Appendix E, focuses on the assembly's reactions to your music ministry.

Selection of Evaluators

This form is designed to be filled out by members of the assembly who are *not* members of any liturgical ministry teams. This provides, in essence, an objective "view from the pew."

No preparation is required in order to use this form. On the day the assembly's evaluation is to take place, the Coordinator arrives early and selects several members of the assembly who are willing to fill out the form. Again, an odd number works best.

Reassure the volunteers that they don't need to be experts. Let them know that there are several other members of the assembly filling out the same form. Point out that all they have to do is answer the questions on the form honestly and turn in the form at the end of the service.

Instruct them to read the instructions on the form beforehand, set it aside during the service, then answer the questions afterward.

Reporting Results

After the volunteers from the assembly have completed their forms, the Coordinator should immediately collect the forms. Before meeting with the evaluated group(s), tabulate the results and be prepared to discuss them.

The Coordinator should present the evaluators' findings to the group(s) evaluated as soon as possible. The section devoted to the Post-Survey Feedback fully explains this step.

As with the previous two forms, repeat this process annually.

Evaluation Form 4: For Music Ministry Team Leaders

Evaluation Form 4, found in Appendix H, focuses on patterns of music selection over time.

Selection of Evaluators

This form is designed to be filled out by the leaders of the music ministry teams over the course of the liturgical year. It records weekly musical choices and provides a way to review long-term patterns of music selection.

No preparation is required. Team leaders simply record their weekly choices and answer the questions at the bottom of the form.

Reporting Results

The information recorded on Form 4 will be kept on file and used during the next annual evaluation process.

Summary

Following these tips will help ensure a successful survey process:

- Ensure that the music ministry teams know *when* the evaluation is going to take place.
- Make sure evaluators have their forms beforehand and know how to use them.
- Remind evaluators to follow instructions on the forms (particularly those that relate to *not* being a distraction during the services).
- Have extra forms and pencils on hand.
- Repeat process annually to measure improvement.

5. Post-Survey Feedback

AS SOON AS Forms 1 through 3 have been filled out, the Coordinator should feed the results back to the groups as quickly as possible. Timely feedback is an essential part of any evaluation process. I recommend that the Post-Survey Feedback Session be conducted *within one to two weeks after* these forms are collected. A sample session plan is provided at the end of this chapter.

Remember, Evaluation Form 4 is not used in the first evaluation cycle. Music ministry team leaders will be asked to fill out one of these forms for each week over the next year. Then these forms can be incorporated into next year's evaluation process. Form 4 is discussed in more detail in Chapter 6.

Sharing the Results

The Coordinator should collect Evaluation Forms 1 through 3 on the same day they are filled out. Set aside some time to immediately review them, searching especially for areas of agreement among the evaluators:

- Where does there seem to be consensus?
- What do they agree the music ministry teams are doing well or doing poorly?

Prepare a summary of the evaluations. This can be a narrative stating what your conclusions are after reviewing the forms. Actually, there are several narratives: one for each group plus an overall summation. Make sufficient copies so you can share the forms and your summary with each group, the liturgy committee, and the pastor.

To help you with this process, a sample of a completed Evaluation Form 1 with summaries is provided in Appendix F. Take a few moments to review the sample; it will give you a "flavor" for the kinds of things you will want to focus on in your summary.

I recommend that you share the evaluation results with the music ministry teams *first*; then relay the results to others such as the liturgy committee and the pastor.

Get together with the music ministry *team leaders* first. Meet with them in the morning portion of the Post-Survey Feedback Session, then have the other group members join you for the afternoon portion.

Your twofold purpose in conducting this feedback session is to let the music ministry teams see how their programs "measure up" to the Standards and to allow each group to create its own plans for improving its ministry.

Making a Plan for Improvement

Groups will vary in their interpretations of what needs to be "fixed" and what needs to be left alone. It's important that the music ministry teams be allowed to decide for themselves which areas are most important and to devise their own plans for addressing weak areas.

It may be tempting for the Coordinator to step in at this point with a heavy hand and dictate what changes need to be made. After all, you've explained the Standards, measured performance in relation to those Standards, and clearly identified areas in which they are weak. Shouldn't you just tell them to fix those weaknesses and be done with it?

Allow me to digress a moment and share with you some painful past experiences in this regard. I did not suddenly wake up one morning and have a clear concept for this book. Rather, I have been a liturgical music minister for some thirty years now, and a music director for twenty of those years, and my experiences (good and bad) provide the foundation for all of the suggestions in this book.

When I first became a director/leader, I had no specific training for leading people and running programs. I was just another marginally competent musician who had a desire to "use my gift for God." I suspect that many readers consider themselves to be in that category.

When I found myself more or less thrust into this position, I soon discovered that I needed whole new sets of skills: people skills and organizational skills. Knowing how to read music, improvise an accompaniment, or transpose a hymn was of little use when trying to run a program. In fact, there wasn't much of a program to run. There were individual musicians and groups holding to their own fiefdoms, and doing their own thing. My job mainly consisted of scurrying around meeting with liturgy committees, determining themes for Masses, then trying to get the various groups to use music that fit those themes.

Over the years, I developed my managerial and organizational skills—sometimes by reading books and articles, sometimes by attending conferences and seminars, and sometimes by gosh and by golly.

Along the way, I sought to share the information I was accumulating by going to conferences and reading important source documents such as The Constitution on the Sacred Liturgy and Music in Catholic Worship. I put on mini-seminars for my own

If music ministry team members feel unappreciated and railroaded into unwanted changes, it is possible that much of the joy of their involvement will be taken away—and that can have catastrophic effects on the quality of their music.

music ministry team members, refined it, shared it with musicians from other local churches, and so on, and so on.

Eventually, I pulled together many of the materials used in Part One, "The Standards," of this handbook. I taught others about the patterns and rhythms of the Mass and how to make music selections that would enhance and complement this experience rather than conflict with it.

As I taught others to do this, I found more and more that I wanted to be able to offer my music ministry team members specific and regular feedback on their performance so that they could improve their selections and presentation of liturgical music over time.

Eventually, I hit upon the system described in this book. But not before I made many stumbling, unsuccessful, heavy-handed, insensitive attempts at imposing this system on others and dictating what they had to change. I even went so far as to tell them *how* they were to make the changes and gave them deadlines to meet—or else.

Well, many a good musician opted for the "or else" clause, and I lost their talent as well as much of the good will of those who remained and chose to put up with my overbearing ways. To those I chased off: my sincere apologies; I hope they found a place where they could more freely share their gifts. To those who stayed: my sincere gratitude; they humbled me and taught me much.

The moral of this story is: Don't try to use the results of this evaluation process as a hammer to force people to "do it your way, or else." They just might opt for the "or else." Even if they *did* make changes you dictated, they might harbor much resentment, which could materially affect their music.

If music ministry team members feel unappreciated and railroaded into unwanted changes, it is possible that much of the joy of their involvement will be taken away—and that can have catastrophic effects on the quality of their music.

Each group will create their own tentative action plan as a result of their discussions of the evaluation results. Action plans can come in any format that makes sense to the groups creating them (a sample form is provided in Appendix G). The point is that their action plans are their own and that they are specific.

Groups should be counseled that they may not be able to implement every thing they'd like to. Sometimes proposals require participation by someone outside the group (like a pastor or music director) who may or may not be able/willing to perform that action. Some proposals might involve money (for such things as training or resources), which may or may not be available. Group members should understand from the outset that their proposals are *recommendations* that may be subject to approval by others.

Action plans will be given to the Coordinator, who will consolidate them and share them with the liturgy committee and the pastor. Most likely, some proposals will be realistic while others will not. Negotiations may be necessary in order to come up with a final plan that enjoys consensus among all the "players" (pastor, liturgy committee, music director, and music ministry teams). When you do reach an agreement, be sure to stick to the plan. The Coordinator should track the agreed-upon actions throughout the year, gently prodding, when necessary, to make sure that everyone lives up to their commitments.

I strongly recommend publishing the final summary, identifying what strengths and weaknesses the evaluation process identified and spelling out the changes that are planned. This will tell the assembly that the ministry takes itself seriously and is attempting to improve what it does. A sample Summary Report is included in Appendix F.

Post-Survey Feedback Session Plan: *First Year*

Preparation

Two Weeks Prior to Feedback

The cardinal rules for feedback are that it must be *specific* and *timely*. Filling out the evaluation forms takes care of the "specific" requirement. It is up to you, the Coordinator, to ensure that the results are shared with the music ministry teams in a timely manner.

This will require some preparation and effort. Collect the forms on the same day they are filled out and immediately begin reviewing and summarizing them. Ideally, you will prepare the summaries in time to conduct the feedback session within two weeks.

Depending on the number of groups evaluated and the number of forms to be reviewed, this could represent a significant time commitment on your part—plan on about five hours for each service evaluated.

It's not that the process is terribly complicated; it's just that it takes time to read every comment made by every evaluator, then distill all of this information into a thoughtful, thorough summary. In Appendix F you will find a sample of a completed Evaluation Form 1 with summaries. This sample is based on an actual evaluation, so it should give you a good "flavor" for how this process should proceed.

I recommend that the Coordinator perform the review and write the summary. It's easier for everyone to "compare notes" if the narratives have all been prepared by the same person. However, this does represent a significant investment of time (especially if four or five groups were evaluated). An alternative is to get the leaders of each group to provide their own summaries. If you choose this alternative, I suggest you arrange for them to obtain the evaluation forms on the same day they are filled out. The goal should be to complete the review and provide a copy of the forms and the summary to the Coordinator by the Wednesday or Thursday of the week after the forms are completed.

Whoever writes the overall and individual group summaries should focus only on those things that seemed to draw comments from more than one evaluator. That is, the summary should focus on the most significant aspects of the evaluation—good or bad—not on every nit-picky comment.

The summary writers should take great care to include the positive comments as well as the negative. Affirm those who give of their time and talent. In general, summary writers should mention positive aspects first, then mention anything that needs to be improved. The examples in Appendix F show how to word the summaries to highlight positive elements. This is critical to the success of the evaluation process. If group members read a summary and see only negative comments, they will find it discouraging. If they see positive comments about their work, they will receive the negative ones more readily and be willing to work on them.

One Week Prior to Feedback

The Coordinator should then arrange for copies to be made of the overall and group-specific summaries. Enough copies of the overall summary should be provided so that "all the players" (musicians, the pastor, the liturgy committee, etc.) can have one. Make sufficient copies of the group-specific summaries so that everyone in that group will have one. There's no need to make copies of the completed evaluation forms; if the group leaders and Coordinator have a set, that should suffice.

When the Coordinator sets up the Post-Survey Feedback Session, he or she should work closely with other parish entities to ensure that the session will not conflict with any other scheduled activity. Arrange for adequate facilities (see the guidelines provided for the Pre-Survey Training Session).

As before with the Pre-Survey Training Session, the Coordinator should *personally* contact the leaders of every music group that will be invited to take part in this feedback session. Phone calls are OK, but face-to-face is more effective and inviting. Print a reminder in the church bulletin.

Communicate that everyone in the group is encouraged to attend because they will be discussing the results of the evaluation and laying down groundwork for changes based on those results. Encourage the leaders of each group to personally contact everyone in their group to issue an invitation to take part in the process.

Three Days Prior to Feedback

Three days before the feedback session, call the leaders to remind them about it, and ask them to call everyone in their group. If you call sooner than that, people will forget it; if you call later than that, they may have already made other plans. Ask for a headcount from each group leader at least two days before the training session (so that adequate numbers of chairs, handouts, etc. can be arranged).

Don't forget:

- Ask the pastor to attend at least the introductory portion of the feedback session.
- Make arrangements for someone to lead and accompany the singing, and find out what they'll need (piano, amp, music stand, etc.).

Secure a supply of pencils and blank paper before the training session occurs. If available, have flip charts or newsprint pads for the brainstorming portion of the feedback session. Ideally, have one for every group. Additionally, bring whatever resources you'll need for the singing: hymnals, songsheets (with reprint permission, of course!), and so on.

One Day Prior to Feedback

The day before the feedback session, the Coordinator should make contact with those who will assist with the feedback session (accompanist, pastor, etc.), assuring that they know where they're supposed to be and when, and what they'll be doing.

The Feedback Session — Morning Portion

On the day of the feedback session, the Coordinator should arrive *at least* one half hour before the participants. Check out the environment (lighting, temperature, etc.). Set up the training area (chairs, tables, lectern, microphone, etc.). Place the handouts, pencils, and other supplies near the door with a sign for attendees to pick up materials as they enter.

Arrange for the group leaders to show up for the morning portion, with everyone else joining you for the afternoon portion.

Introduction

Step 1 *(5 minutes)*

When the group leaders have arrived and you're ready to begin, the Coordinator should have everyone stand and cue the musician(s) to begin the opening song, which will focus and gather them.

Choose a seasonal song or one that focuses on service or ministry—one that they're very familiar with and can join in spontaneously. Perhaps "Service" (Ceasar), "Here I Am" (Schutte), "Servant Song" (McGargill), or "In Christ There Is No East or West" (Oxenham).

I recommend that you sing whatever song you've chosen in its entirety. *Enjoy* the song. *Pray* the song. These are the music ministry team leaders, after all. Let them celebrate their gifts.

Step 2 *(5 minutes)*

Immediately after the song, while everyone is still standing, the pastor should lead a short prayer along the lines of "Thanks for the gift of music" and "Help us to become more faithful servants," etc.

He then invites everyone to be seated, and thanks them for participating in this evaluation process. If he has had an opportunity to read the overall summary, he might cull out a *positive* aspect or two to share with the group, indicating that he's pleased to see it affirmed in the surveys. He should encourage the participants to work closely with the Coordinator to make plans for improvement. He should then indicate that he looks forward to seeing their action plans and assures them of his support in making those changes work. Then he returns control to the Coordinator.

Step 3 *(20 minutes)*

Again, thank those present for taking part in the survey process: filling out survey forms, writing summaries, calling members to increase attendance at training and feedback sessions, etc.

Provide an overview of the Post-Survey Feedback Session, covering the following points:

- The purpose of the morning session is to review those portions of the survey results that apply to the liturgical music program *as a whole.*

- *(In your second and subsequent evaluation years, you will add an additional point here which addresses Evaluation Form 4. See Chapter 6 for the Post-Survey Feedback Session Plan: Second and Subsequent Years.)*

- The leaders will review the overall summary and discuss it in detail, layout out some general plans for addressing broad-based concerns.

- Leaders should take notes because they will be asked to lead a similar review with their individual groups in the afternoon.

- The process will be to read a portion of the overall summary, then review their own group's summary and actual survey forms to see how that element may or may not apply to their individual group.

- Then they will discuss the impact of each statement and what (if anything) should be done with that information.

- After that, they will break, then reconvene with the rest of the group members joining in for the afternoon portion.

Step 4 *(5 minutes)*

If there are any questions, respond to them. Make sure they have writing materials and utensils, their group-specific summaries, and the overall summary.

Step 5 *(20 minutes)*

Read the entire overall summary out loud, asking the attendees to mark on their copies any items that particularly interest or concern them.

Step 6 *(10 minutes)*

Announce a break so attendees can stretch, get coffee, etc.

Discussion of Seasonal Planning Patterns

(In your second and subsequent evaluation years, you will add Steps 7 through 12 here, which address the results recorded in Evaluation Forms 4. See Chapter 6 for the Post-Survey Feedback Session Plan: Second and Subsequent Years.)

Preview of Overall Summary

Step 13 *(15 minutes)*

Reconvene the group and explain the process for discussing the overall summary.

First, the overall summary will be read out loud again, paragraph by paragraph. After each paragraph is read, group leaders will review their own group's summary plus the survey forms to see what comments relate to what was just read. The entire group will have an open discussion about the meaning and impact of each paragraph, exploring questions such as:

- What impact does this item have on our overall liturgical music program? Does it make our program more/less effective?
- Does this item require any action? If so, what and by whom? Is there something all the groups can do *together* or should the groups work on it individually?
- Should anyone other than the music ministry team members get involved with this item, such as the pastor or liturgy committee?

The Coordinator will fill out a Post-Survey Action Plan for each action the group identifies as appropriate for the overall liturgical music program. These Action Plans will specifically state who should do what, and by when? Explain that if their recommendations involve action on the part of other people, those other people may have different priorities and may not be able to do what the groups want when they want. Nevertheless, completing an action plan will be a good way to express what the groups would like to see.

Next, group leaders will take notes on any general actions or strategies that may affect their own groups. Explain that they should be prepared to share these notes with their groups later in the day.

Step 14 *(10 minutes)*

Before beginning the overall summary, the Coordinator sets the tone for the discussions to come. This is a critical step if this feedback session is to be successful. Emphasize that many good observations came out of the evaluation process, and cite a few.

Remind them, however, that the purpose of this feedback session is to identify areas that need work or have room for improvement. Mention that this in not the forum in which to let egos get in the way of constructive dialogue. Emphasize that every group has strong and weak points in its evaluations—and that's perfectly normal.

Remind them, too, that the purpose of conducting the evaluation and feedback session is to "hold up a mirror" for us to see ourselves as others see us. If we are truly liturgical music "ministers," we will acknowledge our servanthood and be willing to honestly look at ourselves and our ministries. We will be willing to change if such change will serve the community by making our music more effective, more prayerful.

Discussion of Overall Summary

Step 15 *(120 minutes)*

Review and discuss each paragraph of the overall summary, as outlined in Step 13. Take breaks as needed during the process. I recommend that the Coordinator lead the discussion, with someone else actually recording what the leaders propose for action items. That leaves the Coordinator free to focus on the group process. Here are some things to look for:

- Make sure everyone is participating. Sometimes, an individual in the group has good ideas but is shy about sharing them. Gently persuade everyone to get involved. A good way to encourage participation is to use brainstorming. Post a large piece of paper in front of the group, ask a question, then go around the room, asking for each person to make one response. Then go around again, asking for a second response, a third, and so on until you've gotten everyone's ideas on the paper. The benefit of this method is that there is no discussion of the merits or faults with any answer at this point—you're just recording them for discussion later. By going around the room, everyone gets a chance to speak.

- Don't let any one person dominate the discussions. If this occurs, the direction of your overall music program will largely be determined by the one who talked the most instead of by a consensus of the liturgical music ministry team leaders.

- Rather than guiding the *direction* of the discussion, focus on the group *process,* making sure everyone is owning the process. Watch their faces; listen to their voices. Are they happy with what's being said? Are they comfortable with the directions the discussion is going? Are they angry or ill-at-ease? Don't let the group move off a subject until you sense they've tapped out whatever they have to say.

- When the time comes to decide what (if anything) should be done with a piece of information, strive for consensus. Keep in mind that you're not trying to come up with a "perfect solution"; you're just trying to identify something that can be done to improve it. You might start out with a list of twenty different things that could be done to fix a certain problem. You might get general agreement on three of those twenty solutions. That's OK. Three improvement actions are better than none. Remind them that these are only recommended actions, which will still need to be approved by others (such as budget and resource people, the pastoral ministry team, the parish council, or others).

Two hours should be sufficient time to work through everything contained in the overall summary. If you find that you are running out of time, don't rush the discussions. Instead, look at the remaining items and pick one or two that seem to be the most important or have the greatest impact, and limit the rest of the discussion to those items. You may have trouble coming to grips with this, but here's the thinking behind it. You're not going to "fix" everything with one round of evaluations. It is enough that you acknowledge areas of strength and weakness and identify a couple that you can address now. Hopefully, you will be repeating this process annually. As the years go by, you'll have plenty of opportunity to discuss the whole range of issues you want to address. For now, be content to identify a couple areas of largest concern and make plans on how to improve just those items.

If you perceive that your overall summary contains too many items to discuss in a couple hours, you can try to reduce the number of items you give your attention to in this feedback session. For instance, you can have each leader vote for which items they most want to discuss. Give each one ten votes and specify that no more than 4 votes can be given to any one item. The participants scan through the paragraphs of the overall summary and mark their votes in the margin. Then you call out each item and count the number of votes it receives. Discuss the items in the order of the total number of votes—the one with the most votes first. There are other timesaving techniques, but this one is quick and simple.

Step 16 *(10 minutes)*

Wrap up by summarizing the items focused on and what actions you decided to recommend for improvement. Remind the group leaders to take these items back to their individual groups this afternoon, when they will go through the same process of reviewing their group-specific summaries. Assure them that you will be circulating around to help if they need it.

Step 17 *(60 minutes)*

Take a one-hour meal break. This is a good time for the rest of the music ministry teams to join you and the leaders to share a meal together. Then continue with everyone's participation in the afternoon.

The Feedback Session — Afternoon Portion

Review of Group Summaries

Step 18 *(5 minutes)*

Reconvene the feedback session with everyone in attendance. Cue the musician(s) to lead a song similar to the one used to begin the morning portion.

Step 19 *(20 minutes)*

Just as you did in the morning portion, thank those present for taking part in the survey process: filling out survey forms, attending the Pre-Survey Training Session and this Post-Survey

Feedback Session. Acknowledge people who took time from their busy schedules to devote some serious attention to their ministry.

Set the stage for the afternoon discussion by covering the following points:

- The purpose of the afternoon portion is to allow each group to review its evaluation surveys and summaries.
- Group leaders will review with group members the results of the morning discussion on the overall summary and how it may affect their group's plans.
- The process will be to read a portion of their group-specific summary, then discuss the impact of each statement and what (if anything) their group should do with that information.
- Any actions the groups decide to take in response to the evaluation results will be recorded on a Post-Survey Action Plan. Some actions may involve inter-group activities; others will concern just their group.

Step 20 *(10 minutes)*

Respond to any questions. Dismiss the group leaders to their individual meeting areas to prepare for their group members to join them. They should spend this time reviewing their copy of the Leader's Guide for Small Group Discussion, found at the end of this session plan. Let them know that, before dismissing the group members to the meeting areas, you're going to cover some background material with them, similar to what you went over with the leaders that morning.

Step 21 *(10 minutes)*

In a manner similar to what you did in the morning, set the tone for the small group discussions to come. This is a critical step if the feedback session is to be successful.

Emphasize that there were many good observations that came out of the evaluation process, and cite a couple of examples. Remind them, however, that the purpose of this meeting is to identify areas that need work or have room for improvement. Mention that this is not the forum in which to let egos get in the way of constructive dialogue. Point out that everyone's evaluations have strong and weak points—and that's perfectly normal.

Let them know that the purpose of conducting this evaluation and holding a feedback session is to "hold up a mirror" for us to see ourselves as others see us. If we are truly liturgical music "ministers," we will acknowledge our servanthood, we will honestly look at ourselves and our ministries, and we will change if such changes will serve the community by making our music more effective, more prayerful.

Step 22 *(20 minutes)*

Announce that they will now be breaking into small groups according to the liturgical music ministry team to which they belong. If some are members of more than one group, ask them to pick one group and stick with that discussion rather than try to shift from one to the other. Encourage those who belong to more than one group to join that group which has less members in attendance in order to even out the group sizes.

Tell them they are to adjourn to their discussion areas, which are designated by where their group leaders are.

Step 23 *(10 minutes)*

Take a short break to get a cup of coffee, soft drink, etc., then begin the group discussions.

Step 24 *(90 minutes)*

In the same manner that you conducted the group discussion with the leaders that morning, the leaders now conduct a review and discussion of their group-specific evaluation summaries. Leaders should make sure to record each action item on a Post-Survey Action Plan. Take breaks as necessary.

Step 25 *(10 minutes)*

When the allotted discussion time expires, announce a ten-minute break, at the end of which all the attendees are to reconvene in the general meeting area. If a group still has unresolved issues and they wish to continue discussions, invite them to do so after the formal closure of the feedback session. It's important for everyone to come back together for closure.

Step 26 *(5 minutes)*

Reconvene the attendees. The easiest way to do this is to repeat the gathering song. Make sure it's a lively one.

Step 27 *(10 minutes)*

When everyone has settled down, begin the closure process. Check out how the participants feel about the feedback session and the evaluation process by exploring questions such as:

- What was the most useful/interesting thing you got out of this Post-Survey Feedback Session today?
- What was the most useful/interesting thing you got out of the entire liturgical music evaluation process?
- Do you think this has been a worthwhile effort? Why or why not?
- This evaluation process works best if it is repeated each year to track our progress over time. Do you want to do this annually?

Step 28 *(15 minutes)*

Explain the follow-up action process. Explain that all the Post-Survey Action Plans will be turned in to you. Each group will get copies of their own plans back plus those related to the overall liturgical music program.

Stress that once an action has been agreed upon, it's important to work to accomplish it. Those tasked with responsibility for accomplishing action items should follow through on those actions and try to complete them by the target dates suggested.

Remind the participants that each group is responsible for completing their own action items. Also mention that those action items that require action by people outside their own group (such as the pastor, the parish council, liturgy committee, etc.) should be considered recommendations. Other commitments, limitations of time, personnel, and budget may affect other people's ability or willingness to carry out a proposed liturgical music action plan.

Finally, announce that one year from now another evaluation will take place to see if the action plans are carried out and to determine if these actions have improved the liturgical music program.

Step 29 *(10 minutes)*

Thank the participants for taking the time to be part of the evaluation process. If other thanks are in order (for food, facilities, whatever), be sure to make those statements now.

Close with a brief prayer of thanksgiving and an upbeat song such as "Glory and Praise" (Schutte), "Canticle of the Sun" (Haugen), "For the Beauty of the Earth (Dix/Pierpoint), "Joyful, Joyful, We Adore Thee" (Van Dyke/Beethoven), or "Sing to the Mountains" (Dufford).

Make sure you have a copy of every group's completed Post-Survey Action Plans, then terminate the session.

Preparing the Final Report

After the session is complete, prepare a final report for the pastor and whoever else needs to see the results of the evaluation process (liturgy committee, parish council, music director, etc.).

The final report consists of several parts.

- First, include a brief cover letter that indicates when the survey was conducted and who coordinated it. The letter should briefly discuss the general group consensus about whether this was a worthwhile undertaking, what went well and what was problematic. Mention also the two or three most positive comments gathered from the evaluation forms, several key areas identified as affecting the overall liturgical music program, and the proposed follow-up actions. Draw attention to any action plans that require involvement from anyone outside the music program (such as those in charge of funding, permission acquisitions, etc.).

- Second, attach the overall summary and all Post-Survey Action Plans associated with it. Do not distribute the reports and action plans that affect specific groups unless you've already worked this out with the group leaders. If you do share these, make sure that those who read them understand that these are internal plans for each group—things they have decided to do to improve their ministries.

- Third, attach a sheet that indicates where everything is filed (the action plans for the individual groups, the completed evaluation forms, etc.). Indicate who will track completion of the overall action plans and indicate if another evaluation will be conducted the following year and approximately when. Close this last page with a brief discussion of suggestions for whomever is tasked with the process next time—facility selection, shortcuts you found, recommendations for changes, etc.

Distribute copies of the final report as follows:

- One should be filed with all the evaluation materials.
- The Coordinator should keep one for him or herself.
- The pastor should receive one.
- Other groups with an interest/involvement in the evaluation process or the music ministry (liturgy committee, parish council, etc.).
- If someone specific has been designated to follow up on the action plans, that individual should get a copy of the report.
- If you feel inclined to share your report with others, please forward a copy of your final report's cover letter to me in care of the publisher's address found in the introduction of this book. Your experience may be incorporated into my workshops or a future edition of this book or similar work.

Leader's Guide for Small Group Discussion

Your role as group leader is to focus attention on what is to be discussed, to keep the process moving, and to ensure that everyone has an opportunity to participate. You will also record each of the group's recommended actions on a Post-Survey Action Plan form.

Review the lesson plan for the discussion. As you lead your group, keep the following in mind:

- Pay attention to the group dynamics and keep everyone involved in the discussion. The more they participate, the more they will "own" the solutions and be willing to put forth effort to make them work.

- Don't let any one person dominate the discussion. Some individuals in the group may have good ideas but are too shy to share them. Gently persuade everyone to participate.

- Keep the group focused and moving forward on the issues at hand. Watch for group reactions. If members are "pulling out of the discussion," it's time to ask them for some input so they don't feel excluded. Watch their faces; listen to their voices. Are they happy with what's being said? Are they comfortable with the direction the discussion is going? Are they angry or ill-at-ease?

- Remember, you're not trying to come up with the perfect solution. You're just trying to identify something that can be done to improve a problem area. You may start out with a list of twenty different things that could be done to fix a certain problem. You might get general agreement on three of those twenty solutions. That's OK; three actions aimed at improving your liturgical music ministry are better than none.

- Remind your members, too, that at this point, you are only trying to identify *recommended* actions, so they should try to recommend the one, two, or three things most likely to improve a problem area. Then those recommendations will still have to be approved by others (such as budget and resource people, the pastoral ministry team, the parish council, etc.).

- If needed, you can take a break about forty-five minutes into the discussion process, but remember you only have ninety total minutes to cover a lot of ground. Keep the group focused.

Step 1 *(10 minutes)*

Read the entire group-specific summary. Your members will annotate their copies as you read, marking those things that are of particular interest or concern to them.

Step 2 *(5 minutes)*

Choose the order in which items on the summary will be discussed. You may do this by giving each group member ten votes. They go back through their summaries and cast votes for those items they most want to discuss; however, they cannot give more than four votes to one particular item. When they are finished with this, call out each item and count the votes it received, totaling them on your copy. Discuss those items with the most votes first.

Point out that in addition to those items from their group-specific summary, they must also discuss their role in certain follow-up actions to the overall summary, which the leaders decided upon in the morning portion. These items will be discussed first, then their group-specific items; in some cases these will overlap.

Step 3 *(10 minutes)*

Read the first item to be discussed. Go around the group, inviting each person to make one comment or suggestion about what should be done with the information; that is, what (if anything) should be done to improve a situation? Ideally, your Coordinator will have provided you with a flip chart or newsprint tablet on which to record your group's responses.

Do not discuss the pros or cons of suggestions as your members respond; just brainstorm. Go around the circle as many times as you have to in order to tap into all the comments the members may have about the item.

Step 4 *(15 minutes)*

Once all the comments on a particular item have been recorded, open up the floor for discussion of the proposed actions. Let your members argue the pros and cons of each one. Try to settle on two or three actions that are most likely to impact the problem area. Use consensus-building, voting, or whatever works to narrow down the list until you have only two actions per item.

Take those two actions and "break them down"; that is, discuss specifically what should be done, by whom, and when. Record each action on a Post-Survey Action Plan form.

Step 5 *(45 minutes)*

Repeat the above process for each item from the overall and group-specific summaries until time runs out. If you need it, discussion time can be continued after the Feedback Session, but at least now you have discussed the most important items.

Step 6 *(5 minutes)*

When the Coordinator calls time, wrap up your discussion. Summarize what your group has discussed and what items you have agreed to take action on. Thank everyone for their active participation in the discussion. Let them know they can get copies of the agreed-upon actions from you after the Coordinator makes copies and puts together the final report.

6. Annual Follow-Up

FOR BEST RESULTS, I recommend that you repeat this process annually. That way, you will have a second snapshot with which to compare where your program is now with where it was a year ago. You'll be able to see the impact that your changes have had, and you'll be able to refine your program year after year.

The best time to conduct this annual evaluation is late September to early October. Summer vacation is over, everyone is back in town, and you've had a few weeks to "settle back into the routine." Whatever dates you select, the important thing is to make it an annual event. The process will become more powerful each year, since people will know that it's coming, will already be familiar with the process, and will, therefore, get more out of it each time around.

For best results, I recommend that you repeat this process annually.

Be sure to report what improvements were accomplished from the previous year's action plans. Acknowledge these to your liturgical music ministers and reward them.

In addition to the annual snapshot offered by repeated use of Evaluation Forms 1 through 3, Evaluation Form 4 offers an ongoing record of music selections throughout the entire liturgical year. This will provide information the other three forms do not address.

Specifically, Form 4 will track how often Mass settings are changed and whether they are appropriate to the season or period of the liturgical year in which they're used. It will record the weekly music and song selections.

One of the goals of effective music ministry is to use quality music more often rather than to constantly change repertoire. That is, repeating quality music is truer to the repetitive nature of "ritual" itself. Additionally, repeating songs of a core repertoire helps the assembly learn the music, get comfortable with it, and truly own it. Repetition contributes to improvement of the assembly's song-prayer. (See Chapter 2 for a discussion of the principle of repetition in liturgical music selection.)

Instruct the leaders of each music ministry team to fill out and retain Evaluation Form 4 after each service they are involved in. When the evaluation process is repeated next year, direct the leaders to bring these forms with them. During the Pre-Survey Training Session, review with the leaders those Standards that address the need for repetitive use of quality music. Discuss with them the choices they made during the year in light of that information to see if they are honoring the principle of repetition or not.

After the first year, I recommend that you require only music ministry team leaders, new musicians, and those who did not participate in the training last year to attend subsequent Pre-Survey Training Sessions. (You might ask everyone to attend the Pre-Survey Training Session once every three to four years as a refresher.) However, every year, everyone should attend the Post-Survey Feedback Session because the content of this session will change significantly from year to year, based on the comments received during each survey process.

In the subsequent years after the first evaluation cycle, you will want to include a module to allow your music ministry team leaders to review their music selection habits from the perspective of an entire season or liturgical year. What follows is a recommended module, which you can "plug into" the Post-Survey Training Session in order to incorporate the additional information provided by Evaluation Form 4.

Post-Survey Feedback Session Plan: *Second and Subsequent Years*

Preparation

The preparatory steps remain the same as for the first-year Post-Survey Training Session, except the Coordinator asks the music ministry team leaders to bring their completed Evaluation Forms 4, which they have accumulated during the year since the first evaluation cycle.

Since these forms are a major discussion segment of the feedback sessions in second and subsequent years, it is worthwhile to take the time to phone all of the music ministry team leaders the night before to remind them to bring the forms along.

The Feedback Session — Morning Portion

Introduction

(To Step 3 of the first-year Post-Survey Feedback Session Plan, add the following point to the overview:)

- Participants will review each leader's overall pattern of long-term liturgical music selection during an entire season, using Evaluation Form 4, which they have filled out at each of their services.

Discussion of Seasonal Planning Patterns

(Steps 7 through 12 are to be inserted in your first-year Post-Survey Feedback Session Plan, before the Preview of Overall Summary. This added portion of discussing Evaluation Form 4 takes about two extra hours, so be sure to account for this when you plan your schedule.)

Step 7 *(15 minutes)*

Review those principles of liturgical music planning that relate to seasonal or overall planning. Refer to Chapter 2, reading out loud the Repetition section. Go around the room, letting each one read a portion until the entire section has been read.

Step 8 *(30 minutes)*

Have the leaders discuss with one another their liturgical music choices for Category 1 (Acclamations) during each season and in ordinary time. Remind them that it is most desirable to use acclamations that come from the same setting in order to maintain the proper balance between Mass parts. Further, it's recommended that a single setting be used throughout a season.

With this in mind, take each season and ask the leaders to share with each other what settings they chose and why. Assure them there are not necessarily any right or wrong answers here. The important thing is for them to discuss the reasons behind their choices. This in itself may be illuminating and may help them make even better choices as they become aware of their contemporaries' decision criteria. Ask them to take notes and share the results of their discussion with their groups (later, in the afternoon portion).

Step 9 *(30 minutes)*

Repeat the above process for Category 2 (Processionals). They may briefly discuss individual selections, but their primary focus should be on how often these songs were changed throughout each season. Did they change selections every week? Point out that according to "The Milwaukee Symposia for Church Composers" (MSCC), changing songs probably does not minister to the needs of the assembly as well as repeating songs throughout an entire season (see MSCC, 21, 30, 34).

Invite them to discuss their patterns of music selection. They should focus on their decisions to *retain* the same song for several weeks, *use it often* during a given season, or *change* titles every week. Lead a discussion on why they did or did not change music during a season, using the following questions:

- Whatever their preference was, what were the results of their decisions?
- What were the pros and cons of those decisions? What was gained or lost in making those decisions?
- Did their choices encourage the assembly to participate more fully and effectively? How?

Again, assure them that their answers are not necessarily right or wrong. The important thing is to explore each other's focus and decision-making process. Why did they choose the songs they chose?

Explain that sharing this decision-making information with each other will help them explore the breadth and depth of the ministerial aspects of ritual music preparation.

Step 10 *(20 minutes)*

Discuss Category 3 (Responsorial Psalm) and 4 (Ordinary Chants). This discussion will be shorter than the previous discussions. Make the point that the responsorial psalm should not be "overproduced" so as to steal emphasis from the gospel acclamation. If the responsorial psalm has lush harmony but the gospel acclamation is plain, the musical emphasis is out of balance. Pose the following questions:

- Did your arrangements honor the level of emphasis accorded the responsorial psalm in relation to the gospel acclamation? If not, what can you suggest to "fix" the balance?
- Was a new psalm sung each week, or did you choose to use seasonal psalms or refrains? What were the advantages and disadvantages of your choices?

Make the similar point that ordinary chants should not normally be emphasized; generally, they should be reserved for special occasions and seasons. However, they can be sung at any time in the liturgical year as long as they aren't out of balance within the rhythm and flow of the liturgy.

- When did you choose to sing these parts? What were the reasons for your choices?
- Were your settings the same as for the core acclamations? If not, why not?

Step 11 *(20 minutes)*

Discuss their choices for Category 5 (Supplementary Songs). The main point here is that there is no requirement to sing these at all. They can be marked by silence or choral or instrumental pieces.

- Did you apply these principles to your choices about music for these moments? If not, why not?
- Are you locked into the "four-hymn syndrome," wherein you feel these moments must be filled with congregational singing every week? If so, why?
- What are your options? Did anybody choose other options? If so, how did you come to that decision?

Step 12 *(15 minutes)*

Wrap up this segment by asking the team leaders the following:

- Are we *collectively* doing a good job of building a parish "core repertoire" of Mass settings and hymnody, which we share in common from one service to the next?

If your group answers "No" to the above question, point out that, clearly, building separate repertoires for each service contributes to a sense of a "fractured community." A common core repertoire can go a long way toward building a sense of unity and belonging within the community (see MSCC, 22). Continue with:

- Can the reasons for not building a common repertoire be overcome? How?
- What can we do to improve this over the next year?

Appendices: FORMS AND INSTRUCTIONS

Appendix A: Pre-Survey Group Member Worksheet

Pre-Survey Group Member Worksheet

How Are We Doing?

Each member of each group should fill out one of these worksheets, which will help to focus group discussion on the issues addressed during the Pre-Survey Training Session. After completing the worksheet, take it with you to the group discussion.

Music Ministry Team ______________________________

What do you think is your group's strongest asset?

What does your group do the best, and why?

What do you think is the one thing this group most needs to focus on, change, or improve? Why?

In general, do you think this group does a good job of selecting liturgically appropriate music and using it effectively during the Mass? Why or why not?

Below is a partial list of the Notes from the Liturgical Music Emphasis Chart, which you studied earlier in the Training Session. Next to each of the musical parts and notes listed below, indicate whether you think your group generally selects music in harmony with these Standards.

Musical Part	**Notes**	**Usually Comply**	**Usually Don't Comply**
Prelude	If used, prefer instrumental.	________	________
Practice	Brief and to the point.	________	________
Entrance	Usually sung; text based on readings or season.	________	________
"Lord, Have Mercy"	Not usually sung; when sung, simple.	________	________
"Glory to God"	Reserved for special occasions.	________	________
Responsorial Psalm	Simple setting; does not overpower entrance song or gospel acclamation.	________	________
Gospel Acclamation	Always sung; more powerful than entrance song.	________	________
Preparation of the Gifts	Usually not sung; silence or quiet instrumentals.	________	________
"Holy, Holy, Holy..."	Usually sung; upbeat and energetic.	________	________
Memorial Acclamation	Usually sung; strong and emphatic.	________	________
Great Amen	Always sung; most powerful of acclamations.	________	________
Lord's Prayer	Usually spoken; simple settings when sung.	________	________
"Lamb of God"	Simple settings; no longer than required by fraction rite.	________	________
Communion	Usually sung; text based on readings or season.	________	________
Recessional	Does not need to be sung by the entire assembly; choral or instrumental OK.	________	________

Appendix B: Pre-Survey Group Leader Summary Sheet

Pre-Survey Group Leader Summary Sheet

Music Ministry Team ______________________________

During the Pre-Survey Training Session, each group had an opportunity to study the published guidelines for selection and implementation of liturgical music.

During one portion of that training experience, you were asked to think about how you perceive your liturgical music group to be doing with respect to the Standards discussed. You and the other members of your group filled out the Pre-Survey Group Member Worksheet and were instructed to bring it to the group discussion.

You will use this summary sheet as a tool to record your group's discussion of each item. This will provide a quick reference guide for you and a set of notes to use when presenting a summary to the larger training group. Use the space below and on the reverse to record a summary of your group's discussion.

Write down the range of answers obtained in response to the questions below and indicate which ones were most "popular" or repeated most frequently, which will help to determine how widely held a particular perception is.

What was the consensus about your group's strongest asset? What does this group do best, and why?

What did members of your group think most needs to be changed or improved? Why?

In general, do you think this group does a good job of selecting liturgically appropriate music and using it effectively during the Mass? Why or why not?

Below is a partial list of the Notes from the Liturgical Music Emphasis Chart, which you studied earlier in the Training Session. Next to each of the musical parts and notes listed below, indicate whether you think your group generally selects music in harmony with these Standards.

Musical Part	**Notes**	**Usually Comply**	**Usually Don't Comply**
Prelude	If used, prefer instrumental.	________	________
Practice	Brief and to the point.	________	________
Entrance	Usually sung; text based on readings or season.	________	________
"Lord, Have Mercy"	Not usually sung; when sung, simple.	________	________
"Glory to God"	Reserved for special occasions.	________	________
Responsorial Psalm	Simple setting; does not overpower entrance song or gospel acclamation.	________	________
Gospel Acclamation	Always sung; more powerful than entrance song.	________	________
Preparation of the Gifts	Usually not sung; silence or quiet instrumentals.	________	________
"Holy, Holy, Holy..."	Usually sung; upbeat and energetic.	________	________
Memorial Acclamation	Usually sung; strong and emphatic.	________	________
Great Amen	Always sung; most powerful of acclamations.	________	________
Lord's Prayer	Usually spoken; simple settings when sung.	________	________
"Lamb of God"	Simple settings; no longer than required by fraction rite.	________	________
Communion	Usually sung; text based on readings or season.	________	________
Recessional	Does not need to be sung by the entire assembly; choral or instrumental OK.	________	________

Appendix C: Evaluation Form 1

Instructions — Evaluation Form 1

This form analyzes in detail each musical moment of the Mass. It is best used for self-evaluation. By evaluating your own group, you will be more likely to trust the results and take action on them.

In filling out this form, please follow these steps:

1. Familiarize yourself with the Standards against which you'll be measuring the performance of the liturgical musicians (see Part One, "The Standards").
2. Read the Explanation of Rating Scale and the Explanation of Line Items, which follow. These will help you fill out Evaluation Form 1.
3. When evaluating a service, sit in an area of the worship space that allows you to experience the entire environment (visual and audio) with a clear view of the presider, musicians, assembly, etc.
4. Be sure you will not be a distraction to others seated around you. *Be discreet, but mark each moment as it happens.*
5. Meet with the other evaluators (if others besides yourself participated) immediately after the service to discuss your observations/perceptions.
6. The results of the combined observations will be presented to the group you evaluated, so the more specific examples you can record, the more useful your feedback will be.

Explanation of Rating Scale

Grade each item on Side One of your evaluation form on a scale of 1 to 5, with 5 representing the high end of the scale.

1 - Implies that the standards for a given item were grossly violated and that the music was a distraction rather than an aid to worship. It would have been better left out altogether.

2 - Indicates that the music had something positive about it, but the overall effect was negative (e.g., the selection was good but the execution was poor, or the execution was great but the choice was wholly inappropriate).

3 - The middle of the scale. It indicates that a musical moment was acceptable but lackluster. It wasn't a negative experience, but it wasn't particularly positive either.

4 - Used to indicate a job well done (i.e., selection, preparation, and execution were all done correctly). The music enhanced that moment in the worship service.

5 - The top of the scale. It indicates superior performance in every phase of preparation and execution. It says that this music was an integral part of the worship service and that the service was made much more powerful and effective and memorable because of the music.

0 - Although not indicated, it is possible to score a zero. This is the case when an essential musical portion of a service is omitted.

Explanation of Line Items — Side One

The notes below are intended to be a summary and guide to use while "scoring" the ritual music associated with each liturgical unit. To properly use the form (and understand the broader context of the notes), evaluators should familiarize themselves thoroughly with the Standards in Part One, upon which this form is based.

Prelude

Generally, in a small church, a prelude is a bit overstated and inappropriate, except perhaps on special days when there will be much singing and other music later in the service. Prelude music should not dominate, nor should it distract the arriving people from visiting and/or praying as they start to gather and prepare themselves for celebration. If a prelude is not used, simply cross it off of the evaluation sheet. If a prelude is used but you find it distracting and out of place, score low. If it is used and done in a manner that reflects the criteria above, score high.

Practice

There should be a warmup of some kind. The act of singing together begins the process of gathering and helps put people in the mood to celebrate. You might sing a song related to the day or the season, or review something to be sung at today's service. Anything out of the ordinary for this assembly should be rehearsed unless it is so simple it can be mastered in a single hearing. The musicians should not try to teach an entire new song just before Mass begins. New music is best introduced over several weeks, played instrumentally as a meditation one week, sung as a solo the next week, the assembly invited to join in on the refrain the week following, and finally used with full participation the fourth week. Three to five minutes should be enough rehearsal time. If the assembly is not given a chance to warm up their voices, or if the rehearsal is poorly led so as to cause confusion or distraction, score low. If it is used well, score high.

Entrance

The purpose of the entrance song is simply to gather the people, to say, "It's time to focus our attention and prepare to worship." The entrance song should draw people out and make them aware that they are part of a worshipping *community*. Remember that this moment is subservient to the gospel. The energy level of the song can be upbeat but should be more restrained than the gospel acclamation. It should be a piece that the community knows well; if participation is weak on the entrance song, that sets a bad tone for the rest of the service. Because it's the first thing the community will be singing, the range should not be too challenging. The text should be related to the season or to the readings of the day. You may have to wait until the Liturgy of the Word to properly evaluate the entrance song (that is, to determine whether it is in proper balance with the gospel acclamation). Score this liturgical unit according to how well it meets the above criteria.

"Lord, Have Mercy"

This should rarely be sung. When it is, it should be simple and unembellished—chanted versions are best. Otherwise, the introductory rites may be too "heavy" with music, and it will be difficult for the Liturgy of the Word to claim its proper emphasis. If omitted, cross off from the evaluation form. If used, apply the above criteria to determine scoring. As with the entrance song, you may have to wait until the Liturgy of the Word to determine if a musical setting is in proper balance.

"Glory to God"

This usually should not be sung. Again, crowding too much music into the introductory rites may detract from the musical focus that should be firmly set on the Liturgy of the Word (the gospel acclamation in particular). In general, save singing the "Glory to God" for special celebrations. Although there are many excellent, energetic settings that may be popular to sing, when used, it should not overshadow the gospel acclamation.

If not used, cross off it off the evaluation form. If used, score according to the above criteria.

Responsorial Psalm

The responsorial psalm is an integral part of the Liturgy of the Word. It has been chosen to reflect the mood and tenor of the readings (usually focusing on the first reading). It presents an opportunity to "feel" what the scriptural texts are saying. Psalms were written as a sung form of communication. Sung psalms are better than spoken ones. Simple, chanted versions are most effective. Overproduced, harmony-laden, chorally sung versions may be out of place if they overpower the gospel acclamation. In general, a seasonal psalm (or at least a common refrain) is preferable over a new setting every week. This reduces the amount of rehearsal time required and lets the assembly participate in the moment more spontaneously. Score accordingly.

Gospel Acclamation

The gospel acclamation should be an attention-getter, a trumpet call to announce that the gospel is about to be proclaimed. It should be powerful. It should always be sung, even at unaccompanied Masses or where no other singing is done at all. The setting should be well known so the assembly can participate spontaneously and with enthusiasm. The assembly's voice should be strong and confident. It should be the strongest piece of ritual music up to this moment in the liturgy. If not sung, score "0". Score high only if it successfully emphasizes and underscores the moment and is clearly the musical high point of the service up to this point.

Profession of Faith

It's hard to think of any occasion where this prayer would be sung. If it is sung, it should be sung by everyone, not just a cantor or schola. The setting should be simple. There are very few of those settings around. Additionally, the time after the readings and homily should be quiet to allow for reflection and preparation for the Liturgy of the Eucharist. It should rarely be sung, and if not used, cross it off the evaluation form. If it is sung, judge it by the above criteria.

General Intercessions

Sometimes the assembly's response may be sung. Even the prayers themselves may be chanted if the setting is simple and unostensible. There's nothing wrong with singing the prayer of the faithful per se, but it has to be in balance with the rest of the service. It has to take its proper place within the ritual. Singing it every week may inappropriately emphasize this liturgical moment. If not sung, cross it off your form. If sung, score high for a simple, participatory setting; score low for over-emphasis.

Preparation of the Gifts

Contrary to common practice, it is not necessary to have sung music during this part of the Mass. The guiding documents are quite clear that this time is intended to be a quiet, low-key ritual moment. It provides a transition between the liturgies of the word and eucharist. It's an opportunity to reflect on the readings and homily and to prepare for communion. However, we are creatures of habit, and most parishes are accustomed to a song at this point in the service. Past parish practice and the preferences of the celebrant should be considered heavily. Although silence may be preferable here, most assemblies will not be used to it and may be uncomfortable with it. A happy compromise is to use this moment for instrumental pieces or choral works. Text should relate to the readings and homily. In addition to judging musical selections by the above criteria, observe the assembly. Gauge their reaction to whatever is used.

- If silence, did the assembly appear comfortable with it, or did they fidget, anxiously awaiting the next thing to happen?
- If an instrumental piece is used, is it reflective of the season or the readings of the day? Does it seem to draw in the assembly?
- If a solo or choral work is used, is it well chosen, and does it appear to reach the assembly?
- If sung by everyone, is this the exception rather than the rule? Is it in balance with the rest of the service, not over-emphasizing this moment to the detriment of the gospel acclamation which preceded it and the core acclamations to follow?

This item should never be crossed off. Score in accordance with the criteria.

Preface

Generally, the preface ("The Lord be with you...") is not sung, and that's too bad. This is where the Liturgy of the Eucharist begins in earnest. It would be entirely appropriate to sing a simple setting of this almost any week wherein other instrumentally accompanied music is used. There are well-known chant versions in the Sacramentary, and wonderful settings have been prepared by Bob Dufford, Dan Schutte, and Michael Joncas (to name but a few). These simple, elegant settings don't require that the celebrant have an accomplished voice to lead it. If not sung, cross it off your form. If sung, score high for simple settings in which the assembly took a strong role. If the setting was complex or elicited little participation from the assembly, score low.

"Holy, Holy, Holy..."

This should usually be sung. The setting should be strong and affirmative and clearly belong to the people. That is, their part should be prominent and confidently sung. Additional instrumentation and choral harmonies are entirely appropriate but should not compete with or drown out the assembly's voice; rather, they should enhance and embellish it. If not sung, score "0". Score high only if it is a strong and affirmative setting, confidently led and accompanied and if the assembly sings its part well.

Note: The acclamations of the eucharistic prayer (the "Holy, Holy, Holy..." through the Great Amen) are "of a piece." They should be seamless; that is, they should all be from the same setting whenever possible, or at least in the same key and musical style so that there's a feeling of cohesiveness.

Eucharistic Prayer

It is wonderful to hear this prayer sung. It is probably unrealistic to expect to hear it sung every week, but clearly, special occasions call for it to be sung if the presider can sing well. However, it must be rehearsed. The accompanist must be able to follow the presider and complement his rendition. If it is not sung, cross it off the form. If sung, score high if it is easy to follow, well sung, and smoothly accompanied. Score low if the setting detracts from the text or if the singing or accompaniment is not done well.

Memorial Acclamation

The instrumental introduction to the memorial acclamation should be brief (no more than two measures, as a rule). It should clearly provide the starting note and should be unique enough so that the people will instantly know which setting is intended and be prepared to sing from the first downbeat. Spontaneity is the essence of an acclamation. The setting should be strong and from the same (or similar) setting as the "Holy, Holy, Holy...." Harmonies and instrumental embellishment are in order when they can be managed without distracting/confusing the assembly. This should be sung even at Masses with no accompaniment. If not sung, score "0". Give high scores only for strong settings sung well by the assembly.

Doxology

If the eucharistic prayer is sung, the doxology (*Per ipsum*, "Through him...") should be sung also. If the eucharistic prayer is spoken, the doxology is best spoken. If sung, it should be well rehearsed so the presider is on time and on key, and the accompaniment leads into the Great Amen instead of clashing with it, overpowering it, or burying it. If not sung, cross it off the form. If sung, score high if it is well sung, smoothly accompanied, and leads seamlessly into the Great Amen.

Great Amen

The Great Amen should always be sung, even when nothing else is. It is the great affirmation the worshipping community makes to the entire content of the eucharistic prayer. Energy-wise, this should be the strongest, most dramatic sung piece of ritual music in the entire liturgy. The assembly should know this acclamation well so they can sing it spontaneously and with confidence. It should be from the same (or similar) setting as the "Holy, Holy, Holy..." and the memorial acclamation. Introductions should be short but clear enough that the people know which version is being used and what their starting point is. Harmony and additional instrumentation are in order, as is repetition. If not sung, score "0". If sung but a strong setting is not used or the assembly does not participate fully, score low. Score high only if this is a musical high point of the service and sung well and confidently.

Lord's Prayer

This should not normally be sung. Using a strong setting of the Lord's Prayer would detract from the prominence that belongs to the Great Amen. If it is sung, it should be reserved for special occasions, sung by everyone (not as a solo/choral piece) in a simple setting. If it is not sung (as should normally be the case), cross it off the form. If it is sung and detracts from the Great Amen, score low. Score high only if it is used occasionally and then only with simple settings known and sung well by the entire assembly.

Doxology to the Lord's Prayer

Although the Lord's Prayer belongs to the category of ordinary chants and is normally not sung, the doxology to the Lord's Prayer ("For the kingdom...") is an acclamation and should normally be sung whether the Lord's Prayer is sung or not.

"Lamb of God"

If the fraction rite is relatively short, and if, as a consequence, singing the "Lamb of God" would extend that moment in the liturgy, then it should be spoken instead of sung. However, in most parishes, an extended fraction rite is observed, and it is perfectly appropriate to sing the "Lamb of God" as long as it does not overshadow the Great Amen. When sung, it should be simple, and the entire assembly should take part. If the fraction rite is short and the "Lamb of God" is spoken instead of sung, cross it off the evaluation form. If a sung "Lamb of God" exceeds the length of the fraction rite, score low. If there is an extended fraction rite and the "Lamb of God" is *not* sung, score "0". When sung, if the setting and length are appropriate according to the criteria above, score high.

Communion

There should normally be at least one communion song (more if the distribution of communion takes a long time). The song should be simple and one the people know well, preferably one in which the people are only required to sing the refrain. That way they can focus on preparing themselves to receive Christ in the Eucharist, they can process without carrying books or songsheets, and yet they can participate in the singing, which subliminally reminds them that we are collectively celebrating the Body of Christ and that this is not just a personal devotion. The song should not be so uptempo that it distracts from the business of processing. The text should address themes such as "We are the body of Christ," "unity," and "family," or focus on the readings of the day. If there are two or more communion songs, the first one might be congregationally sung, the second might be a choral or group piece, and so on. If no congregationally sung song is used, score "0". If they do sing, score according to the criteria above.

Thanksgiving after Communion

Silence is preferred after communion to allow the people time to think, reflect, pray, and absorb all they've been exposed to. When anything fills this space, instrumentals (perhaps extending the musical themes of the communion song[s]) may be most appropriate. If anything is sung, it should be a hymn or song of praise sung by everyone—not a solo or choral piece. If no music is used, cross it off the form. If music is used, score according to the guidelines above.

Recessional Song

It is appropriate for the assembly to sing during the recessional, but an instrumental or choral piece would not be out of place. The selection should not clash with the mood or feeling of the season or the readings of the day. Texts should focus on action (i.e., putting God's word into practice in our lives, living out our Christian commitments, etc.). If the full assembly is invited to participate, the song should be one they know well and can sing with confidence. Whatever choices are made for music during the recessional, score according to the criteria above.

Postlude Postludes are not part of the liturgy proper and are therefore open to whatever creative uses the musicians wish to employ. Often this moment works well when done as an instrumental extension of the recessional music. If the musicians have the ability, improvisations on the theme may be most effective. If no postlude is used, cross it off the evaluation form. If it is used, score it according to how well it seems to fit the moment, the season, the day. Is it a distraction or an effective ending?

Explanation of Line Items — Side Two

Music Selection and Placement Music selection is a complex process. Texts should express concepts, feelings and moods found in the readings, prayers, and the homily. Music should set a tone for the celebration and carry it through from beginning to end. Songs and hymns need to be in balance with the acclamations so that they don't overpower the latter. Selections should be true to the season, the day, and the place they occupy within the service. They should speak to the diversity of those who constitute the assembly (cultural, ethnic, linguistic, etc.). Selections should express ideas and feelings the people can believe in. If they believe, they will sing and more fully celebrate the Mass. Music, regardless of how good it is on its own merit, should be within the competence of the singers and accompanists. When scoring this item, don't base it on any one instance or moment within the liturgy; rather, score according to your overall impressions based on the above criteria.

Instrumentalists Accompanists should be technically competent to perform their roles (sole accompanist on keyboard, member of ensemble, etc.). The accompaniment should be smooth and confident. It should aid the people in their singing, neither overwhelming them nor hiding behind the acoustics of the worship space. Accompaniment should reflect the mood of the piece. Introductions should clearly set tempo and enunciate the starting note. The congregation should clearly sense when they are expected to begin singing. Endings should communicate clearly that the song is finished. Introductions to acclamations must be well rehearsed. These should be short (generally no more than two measures); they should clearly identify which acclamation setting is intended, set the tone and tempo, and indicate the starting note. Acclamations should feel like they spring spontaneously from the worshipping community in response to the moment. Score based on overall impressions according to the above criteria.

Song Leaders

Song leaders should be warm, inviting, and enthusiastic. They should exude confidence. Their voice should clearly be heard in leading a song, yet it should not overpower the assembly. Those with well-trained voices must take particular care not to overwhelm the congregation with the beauty of their voice, lest people prefer to take a passive role and listen instead of join in. The role of the song leader is to encourage the people to sing. Announcements should clearly tell the people what is going to be sung and where to find it. Introductions should be far enough in advance that the people have time to find their place before they're expected to be singing. Song leaders should be masters of body language so that through eye contact, posture, and hand gestures, they can effectively encourage and lead congregational singing. Score according to overall impressions based on the above criteria.

Cantors and Soloists

These are singers who sing solos or do verses in response to congregational refrains. They must be confident. Their sense of pitch and rhythm must be superior. Their enunciation should be impeccable, and their voice should ring clearly and crisply. Score according to this criteria.

Music Ministry Evaluation Form 1

SIDE ONE

Evaluator's Name____________________________ Date __________________

Name of Church ____________________________ Mass Time__________________

Complete the following form. As each musical part of the Mass occurs, rate it using the given Standards as your guide. The abbreviations for the Standards are as follows:

U = Usually sung/played
S = Sometimes sung/played
R = Rarely sung/played

The numerical rating scale goes from 1 to 5, a "5" being the highest.

Musical Part	**Standards**	**Rating**
Prelude	R - Consistent with mood of liturgy. Sets tone.	1 2 3 4 5
Practice	U - Instructive. Short. Effective.	1 2 3 4 5
Entrance	U - Draws people together; makes them aware of unity. Expresses theme. Sets mood.	1 2 3 4 5
"Lord, Have Mercy"	R - Simple, unembellished.	1 2 3 4 5
"Glory to God"	R - Upbeat, but not overpowering the entrance or gospel acclamation.	1 2 3 4 5
Responsorial Psalm	U - All sing refrain. Cantor sings verses. Simple setting, not overpowering the gospel acclamation.	1 2 3 4 5
Gospel Acclamation	U - All sing it. Powerful. Well known/sung. Harmonies, etc.	1 2 3 4 5
Profession of Faith	R - If sung, simple and sung by all.	1 2 3 4 5
General Intercessions	R - Simple. Antiphonal.	1 2 3 4 5
Preparation of the Gifts	U - Usually silence, instrumental, or choral. Quiet. Reflects readings and homily.	1 2 3 4 5
Preface	R - Well-rehearsed.	1 2 3 4 5
"Holy, Holy, Holy..."	U - Strong, driving, well-known.	1 2 3 4 5
Eucharistic Prayer	R - Accompaniment follows celebrant smoothly.	1 2 3 4 5
Memorial Acclamation	U - Strong, well-known. Embellished with harmonies or instrumentation. Smooth, clear intro.	1 2 3 4 5
Doxology	R - Accompaniment follows celebrant smoothly.	1 2 3 4 5
Great Amen	U - Strongest music of entire service, powerful. Harmonies, repetition, embellishment.	1 2 3 4 5
Lord's Prayer	R - If sung, simple setting. Familiar.	1 2 3 4 5
Doxology to the Lord's Prayer	U - All sing it. Should not overpower the Great Amen.	1 2 3 4 5
"Lamb of God"	S - If sung, does not overpower the Great Amen. Does not extend the fraction rite.	1 2 3 4 5
Communion 1	U - All sing. Prefer antiphonal.	1 2 3 4 5
Communion 2	S - Only if long communion. Should not extend the communion rite.	1 2 3 4 5
Thanksgiving after Communion	S - Prefer silence or instrumental. If sung, use hymn of praise.	1 2 3 4 5
Recessional	U - Simple, lively, well-known. Words focus on action.	1 2 3 4 5
Postlude	S - Optional. Instrumental/choral/group.	1 2 3 4 5

Compute score as follows. Cross off line items above that did not apply to the service evaluated. Multiply the number of remaining items by 5 to determine the highest possible score. Enter this number on the blank preceding the words "Possible Points." Next, total the points you've circled indicating the rating for each line item. Enter that total into the blank preceding the words "Total Points." Divide total points by possible points and multiply by 100. This will give you the percentage score for this service.

_______ Possible Points

_______ Total Points

Total Points ÷ Possible Points = _______ x 100 = ______ %

As a rule of thumb, 80% or higher indicates a pattern of appropriate liturgical music selections. A score below 60% indicates a strong need for improvement.

SIDE TWO

Music Selection and Placement		
Selection	Music should relate to the readings/homily/season both in text and in mood/tone. Selections should honor the musical-liturgical-pastoral judgment and reflect the diversity of the assembly (cultural, ethnic, linguistic, etc.).	1 2 3 4 5
Placement	Selections should be placed in such an order as to enhance the natural flow of the liturgy, not disrupt or overwhelm it.	1 2 3 4 5
Instrumentalists		
Accompaniment	Accompaniment should be obviously well-rehearsed. It should be smooth, and transition from one moment to the next. It should lead congregational singing, not bury it. It should be sensitive to the song/liturgical moment/congregation.	1 2 3 4 5
Introduction	Introductions should be generally short, especially for acclamations. They should clearly indicate when the people should come in, and at what pace the song will be sung. When a melody instrument is involved, it should clearly indicate the melody line, especially the beginning note for congregational singing.	1 2 3 4 5
Endings	Songs should terminate well and clearly. People should readily know when to stop singing.	1 2 3 4 5
Song Leaders		
Manner	Should be warm, inviting, enthusiastic. Confident, but not overpowering.	1 2 3 4 5
Announcements	Song leaders should make sure people know what is to be sung. Announcements should be clear and distinct. They should tell the people exactly where to find the song, and well enough in advance that they can find it before they're expected to be singing. For a nice touch, announcements should help set the stage/mood for the song.	1 2 3 4 5
Lead-in	People should see clearly when to begin singing. In voice, gesture, and body language, song leader should indicate this.	1 2 3 4 5
Voice	Song leaders are there to encourage congregational singing. The voice should be clear, enunciation distinct, manner inviting. It should not overpower the congregation, or lull them into a passive, listening roll. Song leader is not soloist. On pitch/time.	1 2 3 4 5
Cantors/Soloists		
Manner	Confident. Emotional content should convey to listeners that the cantor believes what he/she sings.	1 2 3 4 5
Voice	Cantors and soloists should be technically proficient with their voices. They should have good tone and control. They should project well. Enunciation should be superior.	1 2 3 4 5

Please make comments on points not covered above or related to other subjects such as sound system, use of microphones or other equipment, condition of instruments, tuning, etc.:

Appendix D: Evaluation Form 2

Instructions — Evaluation Form 2

Completing this form will provide our evaluation team with your impressions of the liturgical music program from a non-musician's point of view.

In filling out the form, please follow these steps:

1. Familiarize yourself with the form beforehand.
2. When evaluating a service, set the form aside and participate fully in the worship experience.
3. Please "sit out" the service you evaluate. That is, do not perform any other liturgical ministry such as lector, acolyte, minister of hospitality, etc.
4. Fill out the evaluation form immediately after the service, while the experience is still fresh in your mind.
5. Meet with the other evaluators (if others besides yourself participate) immediately after the service to discuss your observations/perceptions.
6. The results of the combined observations will be presented to the group you evaluated, so the more specific you can be, the more useful your feedback.

Music Ministry Evaluation Form 2

Evaluator's Name ______________________________ Date ____________________

Name of Church ______________________________ Mass Time____________________

Answer the questions below and on the reverse side of this form. Your candid responses will help us improve our music ministry program. Please review the questions before Mass, then put the form away so that it will not be a distraction. Participate in the service in your usual manner. Fill out the form immediately after the service, while the experience is fresh in mind. The most important thing for any Mass is that it helps you experience God's presence in your life. Everything must be judged in the light of this success or failure.

Overall Impression

Did this service help you experience God's presence? (Circle one.) YES NO

Why or why not?

What was the most effective part of this service?

What was the most distracting part of this service?

Music

Did the music enhance your experience of the liturgy? (Circle one.) YES NO

Why or why not?

What did you think was the most uplifting liturgical music today, and why?

If there was anything about today's liturgical music that you found distracting or ineffective, what was it, and what made it distracting/ineffective?

In general, did you find the music helpful in experiencing God's presence? (Circle one.) YES NO

Why or why not?

Participation

Did you personally feel invited/encouraged to sing? (Circle one.) YES NO

Why or why not?

Did others in the assembly participate strongly in the singing? (Circle one.) YES NO

In your opinion, why or why not?

Did the music selections seem appropriate to you, given the constituency of the assembly participating in this service (that is, appropriate to their age, cultural and linguistic background, etc.)? (Circle one.) YES NO

Why or why not?

Song Announcements

Were the song announcements clear and correct? (Circle one.) YES NO

Was the music resource easy to use? (Circle one.) YES NO

Were announcements made in time for you to find your place before you were expected to sing? (Circle one.) YES NO

Please add any further comments you wish to make regarding the music at this service:

Appendix E: Evaluation Form 3

Instructions — Evaluation Form 3

Completing this form will provide the liturgical music ministers with general feedback from you as a member of the assembly who worships with us and experiences our music week after week.

When filling out this form, please follow these steps:

1. Read the accompanying form before Mass begins, then put it away so you will have no distractions during the service.

2. Participate in the Mass in your usual fashion. Please do not distract yourself or others around you by attempting to fill in the form during the service.

3. Immediately after Mass, please fill out the form while the experience is fresh.

4. Turn in the form as instructed.

Music Ministry Evaluation Form 3

Name of Church ______________________________ Date ____________________

Mass Time __________________________________

Please read the questions below before the service begins. Put this form aside during Mass, then answer the questions below immediately after the service, while the experience is still fresh in your mind. You will be instructed where to turn in the form.

1. If you found something particularly uplifting about *today's* music, what was it, and why did you find it uplifting?

2. If you found anything distracting about *today's* music, what was it, and why did you find it distracting?

3. Please look around the church at the people attending this service. Note the diversity of this group (age, sex, cultural or ethnic background, etc.). Do you think that, in general, today's music selections "spoke" to them (reached them, were relevant to them)? (Circle one.) YES NO

Why or why not?

4. Do you have any positive or negative comments about the musicians' performance today (including cantors, accompanists, etc.)?

5. Other than today, what do you generally like most about the music and the musicians at this service?

6. Other than today, what do you generally like least about the music and the musicians at this service?

Appendix F: Sample Completed Evaluation Form 1 and Summaries

Celebrant = Fr. D[redacted] Attendance = 400
Accomp. = B[redacted]
Others = Choir

children = 15% | Hispanic = 10%
Teens = 10% | Asian = 10%
Elderly = 25% | Others = 80%
Others = 50%

Music Ministry Evaluation Form 1

SIDE ONE

Evaluator's Name [redacted] Date 4/29 [redacted]

Name of Church [redacted] Mass Time 9:00

Complete the following form. As each musical part of the Mass occurs, rate it using the given Standards as your guide. The abbreviations for the Standards are as follows:

U = Usually sung/played
S = Sometimes sung/played
R = Rarely sung/played

The numerical rating scale goes from 1 to 5, a "5" being the highest.

Musical Part	Standards	Rating
Prelude	R - Consistent with mood of liturgy. Sets tone. [Nice instrumental medley of day's music selections. Done well.]	1 2 3 (4) 5
~~Practice~~	~~U - Instructive. Short. Effective.~~	~~1 2 3 4 5~~
Entrance Notes #1 & #2 & #3 & #4	U - Draws people together; makes them aware of unity. Expresses theme. Sets mood.	1 2 (3) 4 5
~~"Lord, Have Mercy"~~	~~R - Simple, unembellished.~~	~~1 2 3 4 5~~
~~"Glory to God"~~	~~R - Upbeat, but not overpowering the entrance or gospel acclamation.~~	~~1 2 3 4 5~~
Responsorial Psalm Notes #5 #6 #7 #2	U - All sing refrain. Cantor sings verses. Simple setting, not overpowering the gospel acclamation.	1 2 (3) 4 5
Gospel Acclamation Notes 2, 5, 6, 7, 8	U - All sing it. Powerful. Well known/sung. Harmonies, etc. Accompaniment too soft. Didn't lead.	1 (2) 3 4 5
~~Profession of Faith~~	~~R - If sung, simple and sung by all.~~	~~1 2 3 4 5~~
~~General Intercessions~~	~~R - Simple. Antiphonal.~~	~~1 2 3 4 5~~
Preparation of the Gifts	U - Usually silence, instrumental, or choral. Quiet. Reflects readings and homily. Choral solo. Nicely done. Good balance.	1 2 3 (4) 5
~~Preface~~	~~R - Well-rehearsed.~~	~~1 2 3 4 5~~
"Holy, Holy, Holy..."	U - Strong, driving, well-known.	1 2 (3) 4 5
~~Eucharistic Prayer~~	~~R - Accompaniment follows celebrant smoothly.~~	~~1 2 3 4 5~~
Memorial Acclamation	U - Strong, well-known. Embellished with harmonies or instrumentation. Smooth, clear intro.	1 2 (3) 4 5
~~Doxology~~	~~R - Accompaniment follows celebrant smoothly.~~	~~1 2 3 4 5~~
Great Amen	U - Strongest music of entire service, powerful. Harmonies, repetition, embellishment.	1 (2) 3 4 5
~~Lord's Prayer~~	~~R - If sung, simple setting. Familiar.~~	~~1 2 3 4 5~~
~~Doxology to the Lord's Prayer~~	~~U - All sing it. Should not overpower the Great Amen.~~	~~1 2 3 4 5~~
"Lamb of God" Nicely done.	S - If sung, does not overpower the Great Amen. Does not extend the fraction rite.	1 2 3 4 (5)
Communion 1	U - All sing. Prefer antiphonal. See notes 1, 2, 4, 7, 8 Good choral arrangement.	1 2 3 (4) 5
~~Communion 2~~	~~S - Only if long communion. Should not extend the communion rite.~~	~~1 2 3 4 5~~
Thanksgiving after Communion	S - Prefer silence or instrumental. If sung, use hymn of praise. extension of communion song. Good improvisation.	1 2 3 4 (5)
Recessional Note #9	U - Simple, lively, well-known. Words focus on action.	1 2 3 (4) 5
Postlude	S - Optional. Instrumental/choral/group.	1 2 3 4 (5)

[Left margin, partially cut off: "...luia" ... To Joy] / You Are God" / ...week: ...s # 6, 7, 8 / ...l setting the ...aking" / as ...trance.]

65 Possible Points

47 Total Points

Compute score as follows. Cross off line items above that did not apply to the service evaluated. Multiply the number of remaining items by 5 to determine the highest possible score. Enter this number on the blank preceding the words "Possible Points." Next, total the points you've circled indicating the rating for each line item. Enter that total into the blank preceding the words "Total Points." Divide total points by possible points and multiply by 100. This will give you the percentage score for this service.

Total Points ÷ Possible Points = .72 x 100 = 72 %

As a rule of thumb, 80% or higher indicates a pattern of appropriate liturgical music selections. A score below 60% indicates a strong need for improvement.

SIDE TWO

Music Selection and Placement

Selection	Music should relate to the readings/homily/season both in text and in mood/tone. Selections should honor the musical-liturgical-pastoral judgment and reflect the diversity of the assembly (cultural, ethnic, linguistic, etc.).	1 2 3 4 (5)	100
Placement	Selections should be placed in such an order as to enhance the natural flow of the liturgy, not disrupt or overwhelm it.	1 2 3 4 (5)	

Great selections; well thought out.

Instrumentalists Technically proficient. But piano is second-rate, "tinny."

Accompaniment	Accompaniment should be obviously well-rehearsed. It should be smooth, and transition from one moment to the next. It should lead congregational singing, not bury it. It should be sensitive to the song/liturgical moment/congregation.	1 2 3 (4) 5	88
Introduction	Introductions should be generally short, especially for acclamations. They should clearly indicate when the people should come in, and at what pace the song will be sung. When a melody instrument is involved, it should clearly indicate the melody line, especially the beginning note for congregational singing.	1 2 3 (4) 5	
Endings	Songs should terminate well and clearly. People should readily know when to stop singing.	1 2 3 4 (5)	

Add bass player or emphasize lower register.

Nicely played, but too soft.

Song Leaders Great voice, but hidden behind piano. Get out front.

Manner	Should be warm, inviting, enthusiastic. Confident, but not overpowering.	1 2 3 (4) 5	80
Announcements	Song leaders should make sure people know what is to be sung. Announcements should be clear and distinct. They should tell the people exactly where to find the song, and well enough in advance that they can find it before they're expected to be singing. For a nice touch, announcements should help set the stage/mood for the song.	1 2 3 4 (5)	
Lead-in	People should see clearly when to begin singing. In voice, gesture, and body language, song leader should indicate this.	1 (2) 3 4 5	
Voice	Song leaders are there to encourage congregational singing. The voice should be clear, enunciation distinct, manner inviting. It should not overpower the congregation, or lull them into a passive, listening roll. Song leader is not soloist. On pitch/time.	1 2 3 4 (5)	

Cantors/~~Soloists~~

Manner	Confident. Emotional content should convey to listeners that the cantor believes what he/she sings.	1 2 3 4 (5)	100
Voice	Cantors and soloists should be technically proficient with their voices. They should have good tone and control. They should project well. Enunciation should be superior.	1 2 3 4 (5)	

Please make comments on points not covered above or related to other subjects such as sound system, use of microphones or other equipment, condition of instruments, tuning, etc.:

1. Lousy sound system. Too much treble. Feedback.
2. Piano is not a good, quality instrument. Sounds "thin" or "tinny."
3. Entrance: Good selection, good accompaniment (but poor instrumen[t]) strong choral work. Celebrant didn't sing. Few people sang.
4. Need a visible, out-front song leader.
5. Cantor was also accompanist. Great voice, but hidden behind pian[o]
6. Celebrant didn't sing.
7. People didn't sing well (i.e., few sang at all).
8. Accompaniment too soft. Didn't lead. Could hardly hear it.
9. Recessional: Same song as entrance. This time, people sang loudly & with confidence! The difference was that as a Recessional, it was accompanied by the organ vice piano. USE THE ORGAN!

Sample Group-Specific Summary

9:00 A.M. Sunday
April 29

(Name of priest) celebrated. *(Name of music team leader)* and the choir provided music ministry.

Approximately 400 people attended.

Percentage who appeared to be:
Children 15%
Teens 10%
Elderly 25%
Adults 50%

Percentage who appeared to be:
Caucasian 80%
Asian 10%
Hispanic 10%

Great choice for Entrance ("Alleluia" set to "Ode to Joy"). Well done. Good narrative introduction. Good accompaniment. The choir was strong and had clear enunciation. It set the mood for the celebration. Despite all this, very few people sang. This may be due to the need for an out-front, visible songleader, and the choir belting out the melody from their corner may be overwhelming the assembly, making them feel superfluous.

The accompanist did a great job on the responsorial psalm; however, the people need a visible songleader to help them with their part. The gospel acclamation was far too weak. It needs to be much stronger. Use the choir; add harmonies.

The offertory song, "For You Are My God," would have worked well as a choral solo. No one sang along. If it was intended as a solo, it should not have been announced. If it was intended that everyone sing, they've got to get a songleader out front.

The antiphonal setting of the "Holy, Holy, Holy..." used at this service could be made stronger by having the men of the choir sing the phrase, then everyone answer. The memorial acclamation is just too weak. It's far weaker than the "Holy, Holy, Holy...." The Great Amen should be the centerpiece of the eucharistic prayer, but it fizzled. It needs to be strengthened, harmonized, and repeated.

Nice work on "In the Breaking of the Bread" as a communion song. Many people sang it. (It was rehearsed beforehand.) Nice use of choral harmony.

The entrance song was repeated as the recessional. This time lots of people sang it. It probably has to do with the accompaniment. As an entrance song, it was accompanied on the piano, which was just too tinny and weak to really lead. As a recessional, it was accompanied on the organ, and many more people felt drawn into the piece, and the choir didn't drown out the instrument.

Excellent song selection and placement. Great voice for cantor. Very good accompaniment. See comments about piano and organ.

Suggestions: See earlier remarks about piano. They need a visible songleader. The choir should back off of the melody a little bit when only the piano is accompanying. Use them for harmonies and descants. If they're only going to sing melody, pepper them in groups of three or four throughout the congregation to encourage singing.

Sample Overall Summary

Presentation and Discussion of Evaluation Findings

To: *(Pastor's name)*, Liturgy Committee, Parish Council

From: Coordinator, Liturgical Music Ministry Evaluation

Our liturgical music program was evaluated over three consecutive weekends in May *(Year)*. The purpose of this summary is to relay the findings and discuss their significance.

The aim of this evaluation is to represent the evaluators' impressions as accurately as possible and to identify areas that could be improved to make the liturgical music program more effective and dynamic.

The evaluation sheets and their accompanying summaries are attached.

Overall Comments/Observations

1. First, a word about some of the leaders who most stood out during the evaluation.

a) The leader of the 9:30 A.M. Mass' music ministry team is an excellent musician and liturgist. Her selections are impeccable, her voice outstanding, her accompaniment sensitive to the song and the moment. She's a jewel. However, to be most effective, she either needs to let someone else accompany while she gets out front to visibly lead the singing, or she needs to accompany and let someone else do the songleading. She just can't do both jobs the way they're supposed to be done if she's hidden behind the piano.

b) The music leader of the 12 o'clock Mass has a noteworthy talent for music. His voice is clear and confident. His guitar work is much cleaner than most. However, his selections and placements of song leave much to be desired. He contributes more with his voice than his guitar. He should leave the accompaniment to others and get out front where he can be seen to really lead the singing. He's got a lot of potential.

c) The accompanist at the 5 o'clock Mass is quite good. She provides a marvelous instrumental medley of songs and Mass parts as a prelude and a "preview" of what will be sung. I found it most helpful in setting a mood. She also does well with introductions and endings. The cantor at the same Mass elicited the highest level of participation observed during this evaluation cycle. He practiced with the people beforehand. He was personable and "played" with the congregation, pitting one side against the other in trying to elicit participation, to which they responded. However, he has some vocal problems that need attention in order to be more effective. He also needs to make sure that he knows the melody before leading it. In three instances, he sang melodies incorrectly, and the assembly showed some confusion in trying to decide whether to sing along with him or sing what was written in the songbook.

2. The most significant and consistent observation was that there is very little assembly participation in singing. Generally, less than 15% of the attendees were singing at any one time during all three weeks of observation. Some possible reasons:

a) No *visible* songleading. There are accompanists and cantors, but no one is out front in eye contact with the assembly. No one is there to gesture and offer visual as well as aural leadership. No one fills the role of "gracious host" when it comes to leading song and hymnody.

b) The presider does not consistently sing songs and hymns. These are song-prayers of the entire assembly and should rightly be sung by *all* in attendance. The high-visibility profile of the presider makes his non-participation in singing contribute significantly to the assembly's apathy toward singing. A marked difference was observed in the level of participation from one song to the next depending on whether the presider sang or not (e.g., about 15% sang when the presider did not sing; 25-30% sang when he did sing).

c) In some instances, the people may have been simply unfamiliar with the material sung, but it's hard to say since there are only three weeks of observation to draw upon. However, in those three weeks, only one song was repeated twice. In general, people need the opportunity to repeat songs frequently until well-learned. It's not unreasonable to repeat a song-in-the-learning six or eight weeks in a row until the people really "own" it and can sing it spontaneously. If every song is changed every week, the people have little chance to learn the song well enough to pray them—they're busy trying to follow unfamiliar words and notes.

3. Although the selection and placement of music seems competently accomplished at the 9:30 A.M. Mass, in general at the other services, there seems to be little connection between song selections and the readings or season. Additionally, the placement of songs within the liturgy seems to be done rather randomly. There does not seem to be an awareness of the various appropriate energy levels and "moods" of different moments within the liturgy. The songs frequently clashed in mood with what one would expect if the integrity of the liturgical flow were honored. Most of those making song selections have probably not been exposed to substantive training in principles of liturgical music selection.

4. There does not seem to be any overall coordination of the liturgical music program. Each group appears to prepare whatever songs, hymns, and Mass parts most appeal to them. There is little common repertoire shared among the various groups.

5. Generally, the accompanists are competent musicians and do well accompanying hymnody. Those who perform preludes and instrumental solos also do a fine job.

6. In general, songleaders' voices are adequate, pleasant and absent of significant distracting vocal habits.

7. There is very little done in the way of practice or warmup with the assembly. There is nothing to prepare them for their participative role in singing.

8. The single sound system for both spoken word and instrumental and sung music is not ideal. The system seems to be weighted toward the treble end (low frequencies canceled out, high frequencies emphasized). This helps to keep spoken words crisp in the dome-shaped, echo-prone worship space, but it levels out many of the textures of instrumental ensemble and choral work.

The guitars sound tinny, the piano sounds tinkly, the voices do not convey the richness of frequency over- and undertones associated with sung music:

a) Voices and instruments need to either go through a separate sound system or at least through a separate mixer with equalization capabilities to maximize the tonal qualities inherent in sung and instrumental music.

b) When the piano is the only accompaniment instrument, there is a distinctly weak sound to it. There needs to be a foundation to the sound environment for congregational singing. In ensembles, this is accomplished by using a bass. In choral settings, the basses and baritones provide this element. Most keyboard arrangements used at this church were written for organ, not piano. The organ stops can be arranged so that eight-foot and sixteen-foot pipes are used to add depth and foundation to the music (to say nothing of the use of foot pedals). When a piano is the only accompanying instrument, the musician must usually modify the accompaniment-as-written so that the root and fifth can be emphasized (even doubled) in the lefthand to provide a rhythmic bassy foundation. A pseudo-solution is to mic the piano and emphasize the low-end frequencies. This adds a bit of richness to the tone and provides more tonal and rhythmic support to the congregation.

9. The printed insert in many of the songbooks was distracting. It is poorly printed. It is larger than the songbook so that it sticks out of the book in an unsightly manner; it is not attached in any way, so it keeps falling out. Worship aids (including song supplements) should be aesthetically pleasing and not merely functional. They are part of the total worship experience. Mediocrity should not be tolerated; these song inserts are mediocre.

I suggest that if music must be used to supplement the songbook, print it professionally, trim it so that it is the same size as the pages of the songbook, and attach it in such a way as to not fall out.

Appendix G: Post-Survey Action Plan

Post-Survey Action Plan

Music Ministry Team ______________________________ Date ______________________

Group Leader ______________________________

Fill out one of these forms for *each* action your group intends to take as a result of reviewing the evaluations. Be realistic and specific, but try to keep it simple.

1. One problem or area that needs improvement as *we* see it is:

2. We think this could be improved by (specify what needs to be done):

3. Who should perform/follow through on the above action?

4. By when should the action by complete?

Appendix H: Evaluation Form 4

Instructions — Evaluation Form 4

This form should be filled out by the leader of the music ministry team. It is used for tracking music selections over the course of a year, and is designed to be used in conjunction with the annual follow-up process described in Chapter 6. It focuses on broad issues such as the use of repetition, development of a core repertoire, and sensitivity to the cultural, ethnic, and linguistic diversity of the assembly.

In filling out this form, please follow these steps:

1. Familiarize yourself with the principle of repetition and the threefold judgment which should be employed in the selection of liturgical music (see Part One, "The Standards").

2. After each service, fill out one of these forms to record the musical selections and your judgment as to whether the selections were appropriate and effective.

3. Retain these forms throughout the year. They will be used as part of the annual evaluation process to review your patterns of music selection. They will also become the basis for future improvements and refinement.

Music Ministry Evaluation Form 4

Evaluator's Name ______________________ Mass Time/Date __________

Liturgical Season ______________________ Today's Feast __________

In the righthand column below, record the titles of music selections for each category, which are listed in order of liturgical importance. Then answer the questions that follow. Use the leftover space for any additional comments.

CATEGORY **SELECTIONS**

1. ACCLAMATIONS

Setting used for acclamations of the eucharistic prayer ("Holy, Holy, Holy...," memorial acclamation, Great Amen): __________

Gospel acclamation __________

2. PROCESSIONALS

Entrance song __________

Communion song(s) __________

3. RESPONSORIAL PSALM

(Circle one:) seasonal psalm or refrain, or psalm of the day __________

4. ORDINARY CHANTS

"Lord, Have Mercy" __________
Same setting as Category 1? (Circle one:) YES NO

"Glory to God" __________
Same setting as Category 1? (Circle one:) YES NO

Lord's Prayer __________
Same setting as Category 1? (Circle one:) YES NO

"Lamb of God" __________
Same setting as Category 1? (Circle one:) YES NO

5. SUPPLEMENTARY SONGS

Preparation of the gifts __________
(Circle one:) instrumental, solo, or sung by all

Thanksgiving after communion __________
(Circle one:) instrumental, solo, or sung by all

Recessional song __________
(Circle one:) instrumental, solo, or sung by all

Did everything feel balanced (i.e., were appropriate moments emphasized)? (Circle one.) YES NO

Considering the similarity or diversity of the members of the assembly (age, cultural or linguistic background, etc.), do you think that your musical selections reached them or spoke to them? (Circle one.) YES NO

Did accompanists and song leaders perform well? (Circle one.) YES NO
(If not, note problems below.)

Did the assembly sing strongly and well, participating fully? (Circle one.) YES NO
(Comment below.)

Bibliography

"The Constitution on the Sacred Liturgy." Washington, D.C.: United States Catholic Conference, 1963.

Deiss, Lucien, C.S.Sp. *Spirit and Song of the New Liturgy*. Cincinnati: World Library Publications, Inc., 1976.

Funk, Virgil C., and Gabe Huck, eds. *Pastoral Music in Practice*. Washington, D.C.: National Association of Pastoral Musicians and Liturgy Training Publications, 1981.

"The General Instruction of the Roman Missal." Washington, D.C.: International Committee on English in the Liturgy, Inc., 1973.

"Liturgical Music Today." Washington, D.C.: United States Catholic Conference, 1977.

Matonti, Charles J., Rev. *Celebrate with Song...Every Parish Can*. Notre Dame, Indiana: Ave Maria Press, 1982.

"The Milwaukee Symposia for Church Composers: A Ten-Year Report." *Pastoral Music* 17, no. 1 (October-November 1992): 19-50.

"Music in Catholic Worship." Washington, D.C.: United States Catholic Conference, 1972.

Sloyan, Virginia, ed. *Touchstones for Liturgical Ministers*. Washington, D.C.: The Liturgical Conference and The Federation of Diocesan Liturgical Commissions, 1978.

Walsh, Eugene A., S.S. *Parish Sunday Music: The Art of Making Good Choices*. Old Hickory, Tennessee: Pastoral Arts Associates of North America, 1983.

__________. *The Theology of Celebration*. Old Hickory, Tennessee: Pastoral Arts Associates of North America, 1977.